womanskills

woman

skills

EVERYTHING
YOU NEED TO KNOW
TO IMPRESS EVERYONE

ERIN LA ROSA

VOYAGEUR
PRESS

Quarto is the authority on a wide range of topics.

Quarto educates, entertains and enriches the lives of our readers—enthusiasts and lovers of hands-on living.

www.quartoknows.com

© 2016 Quarto Publishing Group USA Inc.
Text © 2016 Erin La Rosa
Illustrations © 2016 Quarto Publishing Group USA Inc.

First published in 2016 by Voyageur Press, an imprint of
Quarto Publishing Group USA Inc., 400 First Avenue North,
Suite 400, Minneapolis, MN 55401 USA.
Telephone: (612) 344-8100 Fax: (612) 344-8692

quartoknows.com
Visit our blogs at quartoknows.com

Voyageur Press titles are also available at discounts in bulk quantity for
industrial or sales-promotional use. For details contact the Special Sales
Manager at Quarto Publishing Group USA Inc., 400 First Avenue North,
Suite 400, Minneapolis, MN 55401 USA.

10 9 8 7 6 5 4 3 2 1

ISBN: 978-0-7603-5018-8

Library of Congress Cataloging-in-Publication Data
Names: La Rosa, Erin, 1985- author.
Title: Womanskills : everything you need to know to impress
everyone / Erin La Rosa.
Description: Minneapolis, MN : Voyageur Press, 2016. | Includes index.
Identifiers: LCCN 2016013559 | ISBN 9780760350188 (sc)
Subjects: LCSH: Women--Life skills guides.
Classification: LCC HQ1221 .L23 2016 | DDC 305.4--dc23
LC record available at https://lccn.loc.gov/2016013559

Printed in China

Acquiring Editor:
Thom O'Hearn

Project Manager:
Caitlin Fultz

Art Director:
Cindy Samargia Laun

Illustrations:
Kelsey King

Design and layout:
Diana Boger

This book is dedicated to my parents,
because they probably bought at least 100 copies of it.
And special thanks to Eoghan. xo

introduction

I've made a huge mistake is a phrase we've all said to ourselves at some point. Everyone makes mistakes, because . . . well, we're humans. Maybe you didn't negotiate a high enough salary, or maybe you started painting a wall only to realize you forgot to put a drop cloth down. It could be that you agreed to host a holiday dinner but forgot to thaw the dang turkey, or that you simply wore the wrong bra on a date and that stray underwire was killing you. We've all been there.

By now you've found life will often deal you a hand you may not know exactly how to work with, and you'll have to think fast to figure it all out. That is why this book will be extremely useful. Don't know how to fix a clogged toilet? Now you can. Want to finally say something to that dude who keeps mansplaining everything to you? Pick from a set of the perfect responses. Need to DIY glitter some heels but are unsure where to start? Grab the supplies from the list and learn how to make those Dorothy-esque pumps your own.

Just think of this book as a fairy godmother. If you have a problem and wish someone else would fix it—poof! The book appears like a wise older woman with a wand and magically helps solve your dilemma. (Singing mice and talented bird seamstresses sold separately.) In short, this is more than just a how-to guide; it's a road map for the rest of your life. Use it to find your way to being the very best version of yourself.

social savvy

WOULDN'T IT BE GREAT if you could push a "charming" button every time you were around other people? That way, your most charming self would emerge when you're faced with a social situation, and you'd have one less thing to worry about.

Alas, while scientists are hard at work on this button, they've yet to roll it out. Which is why picking up some social savvy skills will help you navigate the world of interacting with others. After all, it's important to do more than just show up. You should make other people feel valued when they're around you. That's right, it's time to learn how to be the most charismatic version of yourself!

What that really boils down to is paying attention to details. Like, say, remembering a new person's name. Or ordering wine and looking like an expert in the process. These may seem like small things, but when put together they add up to one truly magnetic person—which is exactly what you are. Whether it's making a great first impression or making your houseguests feel welcome, this chapter is all about the skills you need to be your very best self.

1 REMEMBER A NEW PERSON'S NAME

It was Juliet in Shakespeare's *Romeo and Juliet* who said, "What's in a name? That which we call a rose by any other name would smell as sweet." But if we learned anything from that play, it's that names are actually important. So to answer Juliet's question, quite a lot is in a name.

The good news is that if you're a person who's traditionally bad with names, that's only because you don't know the steps to remember them. Start with the easiest step, which is to repeat the name immediately after you hear it. When people introduce themselves, say their names back to them: "So nice to meet you, Sheila," or "Sheila, I've heard so much about you." Simply saying a name out loud is a great memory device, especially for verbal learners.

If you're more of a visual learner, asking people to spell their names can help you remember them. This is especially painless if someone has an unusual name, but even if it's a common one, you can always play it off by saying, "Oh, sorry, I didn't catch that; can you spell it for me?" As you listen, visualize the letters written across the person's forehead.

Once you've done those things, there are smaller devices to further ingrain the name. Using a mnemonic device with a person's name is a great example of this: "Bill from Berkeley" and so on. Or trying to visually associate a person's name with something, like "Lucy loves lemons," can help it stick.

At the end of a conversation, if these tricks have failed and you've completely forgotten the person's name, don't be afraid to ask for a reminder. Forgetting names is really common, and it won't be offensive when you couch it in a compliment, like "I've really loved talking to you and hope to see you again soon, but I've completely blanked on your name; would you remind me?"

Modesty is a virtue. But you know what's not a virtue? Pouring gasoline on a nice thing that came into your life, lighting a match, and purposely watching it burn. Which is essentially what happens every time you reject or deflect a compliment.

Whether a compliment is genuine or just given to make conversation, learning how to accept one is a real skill. It's not easy because it's so tempting to deflect with something like "Thanks, this was the only clean shirt I had," or unintentionally ask for more reassurance: "You think so? I thought I sounded awful." When you do this, though, you undermine the compliment and make it seem as if you lack confidence. And you, my friend, are a confident person.

So it's time to up your game by learning how to accept a compliment as the strong person you are. When you receive a compliment, look the person in the eye and say, "Thank you." Don't cross your arms, look down, or use nonverbal cues that demonstrate your discomfort. Remain calm, stand up straight, and know that what-ever compliment you get is one you earned. Expressing a simple thank-you acknowledges people who are nice enough to pay you compliments, and it lets them know you're grateful.

GREAT COMPLIMENTS TO GIVE JUST ABOUT ANYONE

"You're such an inspiring person."

"I want to be you when I grow up."

"I think my cat would rather live with you."

"You have great taste in ice-cream toppings."

"I can tell what an amazing friend you are."

If leaving it at "Thank you" makes your skin itch, you can always follow up by letting the person know what the compliment means to you. You could say something like "I really appreciate that" or "You totally made my day," or you could offer kudos to anyone who helped you earn that compliment, like "I couldn't have done it without (insert coworker's name)." Remember, though, give credit only where credit is due, and not as a way to deflect that glorious acclaim.

3 ORDER WINE LIKE A SOMMELIER

Looking over an extensive wine list can often feel like trying to read a language you don't speak but desperately

want to. That language will seem much less foreign to you with a little direction.

As you peruse a wine list, think about the food you plan to order. If you're going to have fish or a vegetarian dish, then a white wine would be a strong pick. For red meat or chicken, reds work well. If you're ordering an in-between dish—say, an appetizer or something containing starches—suss out whether it's on the heavier or lighter side. If it's lighter, match it with a light white wine. If it's richer, then go for the red.

Now at least half the menu should be cut down, because you're going with either a white or red. Glance at the wines you have left to see if there's any kind of pattern—are they predominantly Italian wines, or wines from California? Chances are the person cultivating the

wine list has a preference. By figuring that out, it'll help guide you to choose from their preferred wines, as those are selected with more care.

Price will be the next point of elimination. Think about what you're willing to spend on a bottle, which is roughly four glasses, and narrow the choices down to two or three options from there.

If you're still having trouble deciding, it's time to call in some backup by flagging your server. Instead of asking what the server recommends, ask about the two or three wines you've narrowed it down to. The restaurant may even have a sommelier come to help you with your choice. And chances are good that the sommelier will think you know what you're doing at this point, since you obviously speak wine (wink wink).

4   DRINK WITHOUT GETTING A HANGOVER

Having a hangover is the universe's way of telling you that you don't deserve to drink nice things. Prove the universe wrong!

Drinking in moderation is the easiest way to prevent the hangover drum from beating, but if you know you have a long night ahead of you, a good rule of thumb is to match every drink with a glass of water. So if you've just finished your adult drink, your next order is a glass of water. Repeat, and that will ensure you don't get dehydrated.

Dehydration is one cause of a hangover, so the water should help keep that in check. But the bigger cause is that as you drink you lose a lot of vitamins. To keep those vitamins, opt for juice mixers instead of soda, and take a multivitamin before bed. Even something like a vitamin drink can save you the next morning.

Eating some healthy carbs before a night out will also help you avoid the dreaded hangover. Drinking on an empty stomach allows the alcohol to absorb in your body quicker, but filling up beforehand can slow down the process.

If all else fails, take an anti-inflammatory pill like ibuprofen before you go to bed, if for no other reason than that it will help quiet the universe from saying, "Told ya so" quite so loudly.

5   HOST HOUSEGUESTS

Do they award Nobel Prizes for hosting houseguests? Because they should. Having a houseguest is basically agreeing to a temporary roommate whom you're also responsible for, which effectively makes you a person who deserves an award.

Remember that while having a houseguest does put you out, your guest will also be worried about being a burden. To alleviate that worry, do everything you can to make your guest feel welcome. While you won't be expected to provide room service or gourmet food, asking if there's anything your houseguest would like stocked in the fridge is a nice gesture. It'll also save you an awkward talk in the morning, when you realize your guest is lactose intolerant and you don't have any nondairy coffee creamer.

Some basic cleaning, like laundering the linens and making sure your home doesn't look like a trash heap, should be done in advance as well. After all, the next time you're in your guest's part of town and need to crash, you'd want the same, right? And if this is someone you're close with, adding something extra like a mint on the pillow or fresh flowers on the bedside table will put your guest at ease and show you're happy to have them.

To maintain everyone's sanity, make a copy of the house key. The last thing you want is to get a phone call at work because your guest accidentally got locked out of your place.

And if your guest offers to buy you dinner or do any nice gesture to make up for putting you out, accept it. Letting your guest do something will help them feel like less of a strain on you and make you feel positive about the experience as well. It's only fair that since you're offering them bed and breakfast, they reciprocate with dinner, right?

6 DISCUSS POLITICS WITH FRIENDS

The winner of the "topics to avoid" prize most often goes to politics, especially if you have friends whose positions differ from yours. But politics doesn't have to be off the discussion table as long as you're conscientious.

When you do decide to talk politics, always keep in mind that you should agree to disagree respectfully. In other words, don't roll your eyes, heavily sigh, or grimace when others are voicing their opinions—that's just rude! Let people say what they need to say, and then remain cool as you explain why you don't agree. Not flipping a table or setting the place on fire is the basic goal here, even though political issues can make you want to do just that.

If you decide to bring up a specific topic or point, ask yourself why you want to discuss it. Is it because you're genuinely curious to learn more about it, or you want to hear other people's thoughts? If so, fantastic! But if you're merely trying to win an argument or force people to second-guess their own feelings, this kind of discussion really won't end well.

Then think about whether you know enough about the opposing side's views to argue your own effectively. If you haven't evaluated the arguments made by the opposing side in a thoughtful way, then you haven't fairly reviewed the issue being discussed. Admitting that you don't know a whole lot about the opposition's side is fine; just don't pretend you're an expert on this topic.

Once you've taken all of this into consideration, the biggest question is whether you have solutions to the problem you're bringing up. In other words, it's one thing to debate issues, but have you thought of ways to resolve those issues once you're done with the discussion? If any of the above sounds like too much effort, then you may indeed want to steer clear of discussing politics with friends.

7   COMFORT SOMEONE WHO'S GRIEVING

When someone experiences a loss, it's not always easy to know what to say. Even if it's someone you're close with, it can be hard to fully understand what the person needs to hear.

That's because grief is a seriously complicated emotion, and how it manifests itself will differ with each person. So what you want to do is express your love and support, as there's truly nothing you can say to magically fix the situation.

What you don't want to do is compare it to a similar circumstance you experienced. Each person's grief is unique, and this time isn't about you. Also, saying things like "He's in a better place now" or "It just takes time" can unintentionally minimize the person's pain. And telling people how to feel with advice like "Focus on the positive" or "Be happy for the time you had together" can make people feel ashamed of how they're actually feeling.

What you want to get across is that you're truly there with them and will continue to be whenever they need to talk. Starting off with a simple "I'm so sorry this happened" lets people know that you sympathize with them and are grieving for them. You can follow that up with "If you want to talk about it, I'm here for you." If they do need to talk, they will, and if they're not ready, respect their decision. If you're close, let them know you're thinking about them by checking in every few days. Even texting something as simple as "Thinking of you" can be enough.

8 HELP SOMEONE WHO'S SICK

You don't need to have a medical degree to help someone feel better. Whether it's a passing cold or a life-threatening illness, there are so many ways to offer relief.

Actions speak louder than words, so instead of saying, "Call me if you need anything," go ahead and do something. Maybe it's bringing soup to the person's door or running some unmanageable errands. The point is, most people won't ask for help when they need it, so don't wait to be asked.

If your sick friend lives with someone or has a caregiver, you can even ask for that person's opinion. Asking what needs to be done can help to start a conversation about ways to assist. If your friend has been sick for some time, then offer to give the caregiver a day off. Spend the day with your ailing friend, so the caregiver can tend to personal needs. You'll be helping two people with one gesture.

On a similar note, if your friend is suffering from a chronic or long-term illness, it's important that you show support regularly. Stop by once a week to check in, or schedule something fun like a weekly movie night to keep your friend's spirits high. If you're in different areas and visits aren't an option, then make that person your new pen pal. Providing something to look forward to each week, like a handwritten card, is a simple gesture that will make a big difference. You may not be a doctor, but you'll still be making an impact.

9 BUY THE RIGHT SUPPLIES FOR ENTERTAINING

A karaoke machine, strobe lights, and hired magicians are great, but you don't need fancy gear to have an awesome party. So before you invest in a photo booth, tackle the basics to use anytime you invite people over.

Start simple with wineglasses. You can go big and buy a variety so that if you're serving a red, you'd have a taller glass with a larger bowl (the idea being that reds are bolder and the larger glass allows for their flavors to emerge), or a smaller glass when you're serving white. But you can also get by with a supply of tumblers or regular wineglasses. Regardless, having a set will make any gathering seem more fancy than, say, drinking from a Solo cup.

To keep you and your guests from constantly getting up to go to the kitchen, invest in drink pitchers and an ice bucket with tongs. Fill the pitchers with water, or whatever mixed drink you have, so that you don't have to make each drink by hand. The ice bucket will keep the cubes cold and allow people to serve themselves so you don't have to.

And if you really want to up your drink game, a bar cart is a good purchase for a number of reasons. It will usually have at least two shelves for storage, so you can cart your booze, bar accessories, and cups around. And it's easy to have indoors or outside—so if you and your party move from one space to another, you can bring the drinks with you.

Now that the beverages are covered, it's time to think about the glorious food. The best way to gussy up whatever you're serving is to invest in some serving platters. They'll hold more food than smaller plates and help you to organize what you want to serve, making your food look even more delicious than it already is.

Other things to keep in mind are chairs for people to lounge in. Even if they're just a few folding chairs you keep in storage and only break out for parties—chances are at some point in the night your guests will want to sit, and you may not normally have room for all twenty of your nearest and dearest.

So now you know that being prepared for guests is a lot simpler than hiring a DJ and tarot readers—chairs, drinks, food, and serving platters are all you really need.

10 MASTER TIME MANAGEMENT

If time is money, then saving time is doubly sweet. What's better than having more time *and* more money?

To be extra productive, whether it's at work or on a weekend, start each day with a to-do list and try to organize the entries from most meaningful to least. Once you have that list, it's time to set up a schedule for the day. To do that, think about what time of day you feel supremely focused. Maybe it's in the morning, or in the afternoon, or at night, but that time of day should be the time where you do the things that have the most personal value.

Now think of when in the day you start to lag or aren't quite awake enough. Make that the time where you do mindless things that need to get done, but aren't priorities for you.

So, for example, maybe you really love running. If your most energetic time is in the morning, then that's when you should plan for a run. The other tasks, like sending emails and running errands, can be planned for those more "mindless" times of day.

And don't be afraid of saying no or putting something off if time is tight. Yes, someone emailed you and needs a response. But is that response needed right at this moment? If not, then ignore it until you actually have some of that mindless time at your disposal.

If your schedule isn't cutting it, then decide what the number one thing to you is at this moment. Cleaning out your closet? Finally reading that book? Ordering delivery food? Whatever it is, carve out time for that one thing in the day and make sure you devote yourself to it.

11   BECOME A MORNING PERSON

Carpe diem. Seize the day! Or, failing that, at least learn how to trick yourself into becoming more of a morning person so you don't wake up wanting to scream at people.

This is going to seem obvious, but the first step to becoming a morning person is to get enough sleep. Logging the recommended seven to nine hours a night will make waking up feel a lot less painful. Routine also helps, so keep the time you roll out of bed each morning consistent if you can. Having trouble sleeping, you say? Remove distractions, such as the computer, TV, and phone, from your bedroom. Make that room a sacred place, and get your body into the habit of sleeping in your bedroom (you know, rather than texting all night).

Since hitting the snooze button can be so tempting, put your alarm in a place where you have to stand up to turn it off. It's easy to roll over and go back to sleep if the alarm is within reach, but not so much if you've already woken yourself up. And the alarm doesn't have to be a grating beeping noise—choose a sound that won't make you want to cry every time you hear it.

Once you're up, drink a full glass of water. Overnight your body can get dehydrated, and when you're dehydrated, you feel tired. So fill up on water to wake yourself up.

And if you really need some motivation, don't be afraid to treat yourself. Maybe it's a fresh cup of coffee or taking a longer shower than you normally would, but rewards work. So reward yourself silly until you're the morning person you never knew you wanted to be.

Horrifying fact of the day: it takes only about a minute for another person to get an impression of you. The good news is, whether you're walking into a job interview or a party, there are plenty of ways to make sure your first impression is the right one.

Remember that most people are just as uncomfortable as you are when meeting someone for the first time. So go into situations thinking less about how you can be more comfortable, and think instead about how to make others feel relaxed. Initiate questions, smile, and be engaged in the conversation. If others feel comfortable, chances are they'll remember you as the nice person who made them feel at ease.

If you're going into a job interview, do research and prepare some potential questions beforehand. Even if you're just researching the company and not the person you're meeting, it'll still give you a conversation opener, like "I was so pleased to hear about your recent merger. How's it been so far?" Plus, being prepared is always a solid way to make a good first impression.

Another tip (that is admittedly superficial) is to think about what you want to wear before this meeting. What you wear in life often dictates your level of confidence. You're probably going to be significantly more self-assured wearing your favorite pair of jeans than you are in a tight pencil skirt you bought the day before. So if you have the option to wear whatever you want, think about what will make you feel composed. That way you can present your most confident self, and others will be drawn to you.

And since starting a conversation is often one of the first steps to a great impression, giving someone else a compliment is an easy way in. If you see the host of a party, for example, use something like "You have such an amazing home" to get you started. To keep that conversation going, remember that every time someone asks you a question, you can bounce it back with "What about you?" Yes, it only takes a minute for someone to get an impression of you, but with the right tools that minute will fly by.

13 RESPOND TO MANSPLAINING

Mansplaining: when a man explains something to you that you may already be an expert on, in a way that's totally patronizing. While most men don't do it intentionally, that doesn't mean you have to keep quiet about it when it happens.

For starters, assess your relationship with the person. If he's your boss, for example, the mansplaining may be harder to address than, say, if he's a friend you've known forever. If he's someone with whom you have a more formal relationship, then ignoring it is fine. Mansplainers are the dumb ones, not you, and you don't need to sink to their level.

If you do feel like pushing back, though, a good way to do that is to closely repeat the mansplained thing. For example, if you say you're hungry, and the mansplainer says, "You can't be hungry after all that food," you can repeat, "No, you think I can't be hungry, but I'm hungry." Or you could pick apart what he's just said by asking, "Why would you think I couldn't possibly be hungry? How did you come to that conclusion?" Making his offhand or casual mansplaining uncomfortable is the ultimate goal here.

When you're mansplained to by a total stranger, or someone you feel comfortable calling out, then by all means call him out! If you need help with wording, try a simple "Yes, I already know how to do that. I don't need

you to explain it to me," or a bold "I don't need you to mansplain my feelings. I know exactly how I feel."

The main point here is that mansplaining is never OK, and if you want to react to it, you absolutely can. Here are some more ways to react, if you need inspiration:

"Why do you assume I don't already know this?"

"My experience is my own, and you don't know anything about it."

"Don't dismiss my feelings, jerkdog."

"Let me stop you there, because you're mansplaining, and I don't consort with your kind."

"No one wants to hear anything more from you, mansplainer."

Nobody puts Baby (AKA you) in the corner. Except when you're in a bad mood, and all you want to do is find a corner so you can close the curtains, lock the door, and throw your phone across the room. While a bad mood is totally acceptable, there are times when being in a funk isn't ideal. Maybe you have a big meeting at work or need to attend a party where you'll have to be "on." Regardless of why you need to break your bad mood, there are ways to do it.

Listening to upbeat or calming music for ten minutes is scientifically proven to reduce stress levels and lower your blood pressure, so crank up the tunes. And while you're at it, head outside—to the park, beach, you name it. Being in nature, much like listening to music, has been shown to help bring most people to a more centered and calm place.

If you have the time, try doing something nice for someone else. Maybe it's paying for someone's coffee or sending a really thoughtful text to a friend. Regardless, it

will brighten your mood to know you've made someone else's day a little less stressful.

Or if you're feeling gloomy because you're bogged down with things you need to do, write out a to-do list and take time to cross out one or two items. Knowing that it's all written out will take the burden out of your head and put it onto the paper. And crossing off even one item will remind you that these are problems you can solve with a little time.

If none of the above works for you, then indulge your bad mood. Let yourself *really* feel all of the emotions you're wading through. Maybe you need to write down everything that's pissing you off, vent to your mom, or scream it out. Whatever you do, the goal is to let the bad mood wash over you so you can then fully let it go. Sometimes you just need to ride the bad mood out, and that's OK. If, however, you're unable to simply let it go and the bad mood seems to be permanent, then know that seeking help is the best option. Because there's a difference between a few bad days and feeling that way most of the time, and what's important to know is that you're not alone.

If you have a friend who makes you feel like you just got hit by a truck after every encounter, then you likely have a toxic friendship on your hands. Maybe the relationship is all take and no give, or the person brings out the worst in you, but letting go of that relationship will help you move in a positive direction.

It's completely under your control as to whether this person stays in your life. So consider the friendship and decide whether or not this is a funk your friend will come out of and if you can wait for that to happen. If you decide that the person adversely affects you, and you're no longer in denial, then it's time to let go.

If you don't ever want to see this person again, then be upfront about it. Don't get in your friend's face or play the blame game. This is your opportunity to sever contact with a person who's negatively impacting your life, so be direct and brutally honest when explaining why you need to leave this friendship.

However, if you know you'll have to see this person again at some point, begin by slowly pulling away. Say no to hanging out, and if you know your friend will be somewhere, don't feel obligated to go. Removing yourself from situations where the person can hurt you will show that you're no longer available for the drama.

Regardless of which approach you take, it's important to fill the hole of lost friendship with something positive. Surround yourself with more supportive people and experiences. Whatever part of yourself this person emptied, fill it back up with what you'd prefer to have had during that time. Having a toxic friend can be a temporary blip in your life, but it's up to you to make the change.

It's a truth universally acknowledged that the older you get, the harder it is to make friends. Maybe it's because we don't have that wonderful playground setting to find like-minded mates to go down the slide with. Still, even without a playground, it's possible.

First and foremost, be yourself. Trying to reinvent yourself or play a part when meeting a new potential friend won't help you in the long run. If a person doesn't get along with you being you, then that person's not the kind of long-term friend you want to have. Related: if you pursue a hobby you actually enjoy, you're more likely to meet someone compatible with you.

Another idea is a "friend date." This is when you ask a current friend to set you up on a blind "date" (or even a group date) with a potentially compatible friend. Yes, that means you may have to be a little vulnerable to do the asking, but that's a large part of what making new friends is about—being vulnerable to another person.

Once you've met a potential new friend, be consistent with that friendship. You could go to a yoga class every Saturday or brunch once every two weeks. It could be anything! Just choose something you enjoy that will also set a pattern of hanging out.

It's also good to keep in mind that making new friends doesn't have to mean making a bunch of new friends. You can gain a lot from finding just one person to talk to and hang out with. If that person becomes a true friend, you'll meet more new people through your new friend, and your circle will inevitably widen.

17 BE A GOOD FRIEND

If there were an app your friends could use to rate you on a scale from one to ten, what number do you think you'd get? If it's not close to a ten, then it's time to take your friend skills to the next level.

One way to show what a dedicated pal you are is to stand up for your friends when they need it. Say they're having a really rough patch. While that's awful for them, it also gives you the chance to be their personal coach and get their head back in the game. Similarly, if someone says something about your friends behind their backs, don't stay silent. Always be willing to come to a friend's defense. (Chances are if you're their champion, they'll be yours when you need it too.)

Another way to earn friend points is to celebrate your friends' successes, even when you might be a little jealous of them. When good things happen for your friends, remember that the moment is about them and not about you. Hide whatever jealousy you might feel and take the time to congratulate them. Hell, maybe even buy them a drink!

On the other hand, when friends tell you their problems, try listening first instead of jumping straight into giving advice. The point of a friendship is to have an equal relationship, and that doesn't fit well with constant lecturing. If your friends need your opinion, they'll ask for it. When confronted with a friend's problem, start with something like "That sounds terrible. How are you doing?"

One important related point: since listening takes time, it's important to actually make time for your friends. This may seem like an obvious friend thing to do, but it's something that becomes harder as you get older. If you don't work or live with your friends, you may settle into the habit of just not seeing them as much. Set up a schedule, a weekly meetup, or just be better about texting friends out of the blue—the more you make them a priority, the more they'll make you a priority as well.

18 TAKE MORE RISKS

Not all risks are worth taking—for example, the risk of leaving the pizza box unguarded and someone getting the last slice before you—but some risks are. Like leaving a bad job for a potentially better one. Or ending a bad relationship because you think someone better suited could be right around the corner.

To stop being afraid of risks and start embracing them, you should remember that when you take a risk, there's always the option of backing out. Knowing that you can quit at any time will give you the courage to at least try. OK, so you've decided to take a new job, but within the first week you have a terrible feeling about the work place. No big deal; start looking for new jobs right away, and don't be afraid to leave the situation.

This is easier said than done, but you can build up more confidence in yourself so that you can be positive about the risk you're taking. Do that by writing a pros-only list, no cons, to really clarify the positives of the risk. Also, tell yourself that you can do this. Take time to rehearse how the risk will go in your head over and over until you can really see the positives at the end of the risk tunnel.

Other things that will help you to take a big risk are to not put everything on the line. If your risk could literally destroy your life (like quitting your job without having any savings), then don't do it. That's simply not a risk worth taking. Just start by taking risks that you can bounce back from if they don't work out, and they'll seem a lot less daunting. And instead of taking multiple risks at a time, start with one. Once you see how easy and powerful that one risk can be, taking more won't seem so difficult.

19 USE POSITIVE BODY LANGUAGE

Even when you think you're saying nothing—because you're literally silent—your body language is still talking for you. That's why you should become fluent in your body's language to make sure it's sending the right message.

Start with your posture. You want to stand up straight, but not rigid, and relax your shoulders. If you have trouble nailing the whole "straight but relaxed" thing, then roll your shoulders out a couple of times to help your body transition into it. Before you know it, you'll be effortlessly tall with an air of calm.

And when you're talking to people, align your body with theirs so you're facing them completely, which helps you seem engaged. This can also be done when you're seated; just make sure your body isn't angled away from them. The goal is to have your focus on them, and in that way you're projecting positivity.

Similarly, work on your eye contact. When people are talking to you, or you're talking to them, you should be looking them in the eyes. That doesn't mean staring them down, but you want to let them know you're

listening with your eyes. So blink when you need to, and look away from time to time, but maintain eye contact throughout a conversation. It may seem a little unnatural at first, but once people realize you're engaged with what they're saying, you'll both feel a lot more relaxed.

Another easy fix is how you're using your arms. Putting your hands in front of your mouth, or on your face, can signal insecurity. And holding something in front of you, like a cup of coffee, creates an unintentional barrier between you and other people. So get comfortable with hanging your arms at your side or tucking your hands into your pockets. Either way, you want your body to appear more open to the conversation and less closed off, because even if you're just listening, you're still sending a very loud and clear message.

20 SORT OUT A TIP

Here's a tip: be the kind of woman who generously tips and not the kind whom servers dread.

The first step to becoming the better woman is to understand that it's not acceptable to not tip a server. Servers in the United States make their livelihood from tips, and to not tip dips into their ability to live their lives. If the service is poor, ask to see the manager and explain the issues. Chances are you'll get a discounted meal, and regardless of what happens, you should still leave a tip.

So, how much to tip? In the United States, 20 percent is a generous tip, though it's acceptable to leave 15. If you're not ordering food, just drinks, then tipping $1 per drink is acceptable.

To avoid constantly pulling out your phone to figure out what the tip should be, there are a few tricks to guide how much to tip, like the decimal trick, where you take the pretax total and move the decimal. So, for a bill that's $35.55, to get a 20 percent tip, you'd move the decimal once to the left to get $3.555, then round up to an easier figure, $3.60, and double that amount to get your tip, $7.20.

Some people try to calculate the bill using the tax, but remember that tax varies by state. This method may cause you to underpay, so sort out the bill through the decimal method instead. That way you can keep leaving tips and never risk becoming *that* customer.

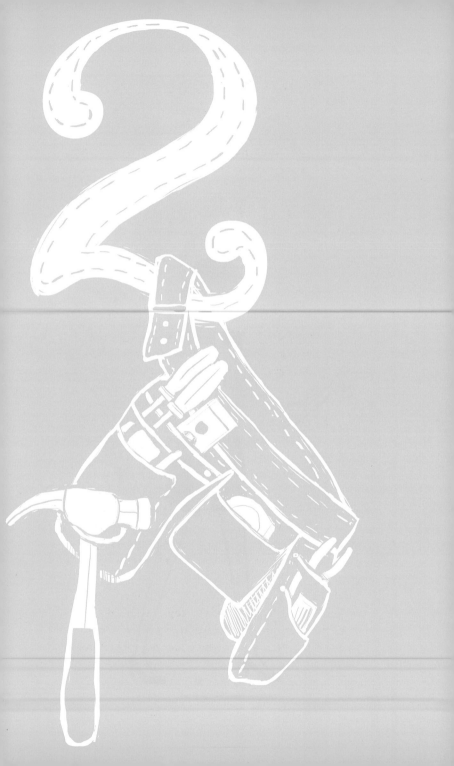

home sweet home

HOME IS WHERE THE HEART IS. But it's also where your clothes, food, shoes, books, plates, snacks, and TV are. So, really, home is where all the good stuff is.

Some of us spend a lot of time at home—these people are called homebodies, and they make excellent dates for a movie night. Meanwhile, others only pop in at home to sleep. Regardless of which camp you fall into, you probably don't want to be residing in a hellhole. (Hellholes are lame, unlivable places.) The good news is that if your home is a hellhole, you can turn it into a truly magical part of the world. And even if you're an at-home pro, there's always room for improvement. Whether it's gussying things up by hanging framed art or restyling your sofa, you can make your home the very best place to be.

At some point, you may even want to invite people over. So it's important that those people feel comfortable in your place rather than feel the need for a long shower after they leave. That means knowing how often to clean and what to clean with, along with mastering the subtle art of unclogging the toilet when necessary.

Luckily, after reading this chapter, you'll be able to do all of the above and more. (*More* meaning things like painting a room and not ending up with splashes all over your carpet.) So strap on your tool belt, and get ready to transform your home into a mini-oasis.

1 BUILD A TOOLBOX

Who needs to hire a handyman when you can be your own handywoman? Keeping the essential tools around your house will ensure you're never without help (from yourself) again.

Let's begin by gathering the fundamentals. Start with a tape measure and level, both of which will help when you're trying to mount objects around your house (and

guarantee they don't fall off the wall). A screwdriver set that comes with both Phillips and flathead types is going to be invaluable for adjusting the little things. Next you'll want to invest in a good utility knife—it can do everything from opening a box to trimming the edges of your drawer liner. And you'll need a pair of pliers for any hard-to-grip surfaces you have to deal with. Then there's a stepladder, which may not exactly fit into that toolbox but will be the thing that saves you from trying to scale a bookshelf to nail in a picture frame. Last but not least of the basics is a hammer—which you can use to secure a nail or just hang from your tool belt so you can look like a casual yet handy woman.

Now on to the power tools, because more power is always a good thing. An electric drill is exactly like a screwdriver, except it takes way less time to do the same job. So if you keep this close, it'll free you up to go out and live your best life. A staple gun is another power tool to consider for your arsenal because of its versatility. If you're into crafting, a staple gun can help for things like upholstery projects, but it's also great for practical stuff, like when you need to replace a doorframe.

With these items in your toolkit, you can say, "Screw the handyman" and safely screw in your own shelves.

2 ASSEMBLE A NATURAL DISASTER KIT

Just as Forrest Gump's momma said, life is like a box of chocolates, and you truly never know what you're going to get. You may get a carefree existence, or you might get a tornado. Since we never know what life has in store for us, having a disaster kit in your home will ensure you're prepared for whatever pops up.

Food and water are the obvious things you'll need in your kit. You should have at least three days' worth of both, and account for a gallon of filtered and packaged water a day per person. Sports recovery drinks are also a good idea, since you'll likely be expending more energy than normal. For the same reason, your kit should include plenty of nonperishables and high-protein foods. Peanut butter, nuts, protein bars, dried fruits, and canned chili are just a few items to include in your kit.

Because all kinds of things can happen in a disaster situation, have a solid first-aid kit on hand. You'll want adhesive bandages, gloves, sterile bandages, antibiotic towelettes, a thermometer, and burn ointment. Those will help keep you alive, but you'll also want other supplies, like candles, matches, a sewing kit, tweezers, a flashlight, batteries, a knife, a can opener, and a battery-powered radio.

If you have any prescription meds you'd need, make sure you have enough on hand to last you through a solid three days (which is how long it could take a rescue team to find you in a disaster situation). And keep other items, like garbage bags and sanitizers, on hand to make sure you're staying clean and safe.

3 ## USE A HAMMER WITHOUT WHACKING YOUR THUMB

You don't have to watch your life flash before your eyes every time you nail something to a wall. There are ways around beating yourself up.

Try putting a nail through a piece of cardboard first. Once the nail is in the cardboard, you can hold up the cardboard and hit the nail until it's secured in the wall. When you're ready to remove the cardboard, just tear it away.

Or if you have your handywoman toolbox at the ready, a pair of needle-nose pliers can hold the nail as a stand-in

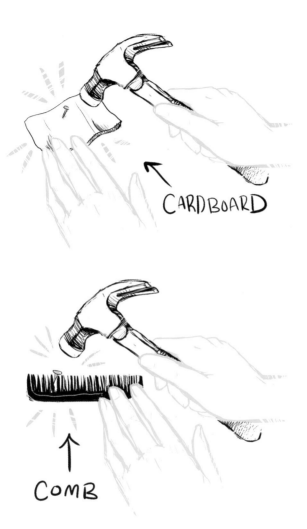

CARDBOARD

COMB

for your hand. Since you hold the bottom of the pliers, the hammer will tap the nail in without tapping you.

When all else fails, if the nail is small enough, you can wedge it into the teeth of a cheap plastic comb. Just hold the edge of the comb and hammer away. No need to sweat the threat of a broken thumb.

In terms of things that can come between you and a hot shower, your own hair shouldn't be one of them. Unfortunately, chemical products rarely get rid of a blockage—and they're bad on the pipes and environment—so put down the liquid and graduate to snaking the drain.

To snake a drain you can either buy an auger—commonly known as a snake—or make a DIY minisnake. For the DIY version, which is far less bulky, go to the hardware store and buy a few feet of one-eighth-inch stainless-steel cable. Take the end of the cable and, using a pair of needle-nose pliers from your handywoman tool belt, bend a few wires (the small, individual parts of a single strand that comprises the cable) in various directions. That way when you work the minisnake down the drain, those wires can snag the hair out.

Whether using an auger or minisnake, you'll want to start by removing the stopper from your tub or sink and any hair that comes out with it. Then take your tool

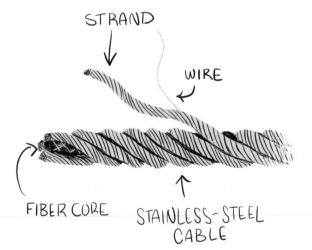

STRAND

WIRE

FIBER CORE

STAINLESS-STEEL CABLE

and feed the end of it into the drain, twisting as you gently move in. When you hit the clog, you'll feel resistance. If you're using the minisnake, start to twist once you feel the clog, and slowly extract the cable and the hair. You may have to repeat this up to three times until the blockage is totally gone.

Similarly, when you feel the clog with the auger, you'll rotate the auger against the blockage until the blockage is released and the auger can go cleanly through the drain. If you continue to feel resistance even after several rotations, pull the auger out and clear away any parts of the clog it caught. You can repeat this until the auger goes cleanly through the pipe.

To finish, all you have to do is run some water and step into the shower with the pride of knowing that you saved the day (and the drain).

5 UNCLOG A TOILET

Rare is the toilet clog that happens when you're home alone and have nothing better to do. Common is the clog that appears when you've invited a lot of people over, and they all have to use the bathroom at once. Awesome. But what clogs don't know is that you're wise to their ways, and you know how to nix them.

The first thing you want to do is keep the toilet from overflowing. So instead of trying to flush everything down, don't continue to flush if you see that there's a clog. Take the lid off the tank and close the toilet flapper so water can't continue to be funneled in. Once you've ensured there's no overflow, grab newspapers or paper towels to line the floor in case any spillage or splashes occur. This will make cleanup exponentially easier in the long run.

If you can see the cause of the clog—say, a kid decides to try to flush a toy—put on a pair of rubbers (gloves, you

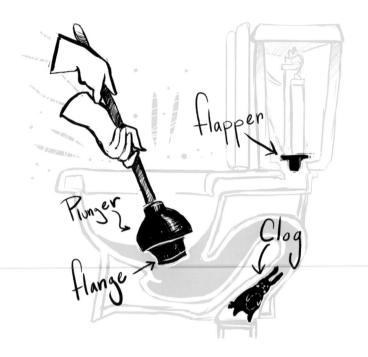

flapper

Plunger

Clog

flange

pervs), and reach into the bowl to remove it. It's gross, yes, but necessary.

If you can't remove the source or see it, it's time to get to plunging. The thing about plungers is that quality really does matter here—so don't skimp and opt for a cheap one. You want a plunger with suction that will actually help when you need to remove an obstruction. Look for a plunger that's ball-shaped or has a rubber flange at the bottom, as these types are best for suction.

Now that you have the plunger, insert it into the toilet and directly over the hole. You'll want to pump the plunger over the hole by quickly pushing down then pulling up to loosen the clog. Eventually, the water should start to drain—it may take up to fifteen plunges—and the toilet will be effectively unclogged. But if it isn't, you know who to call: The Plumber (and not the Ghostbusters!).

We women are heroes pretty much every day of our lives. And there's no telling when our heroism will be needed. Maybe your friend goes a little crazy with the candles, or you realize there's actually metal on that container you popped into the microwave. Whatever the situation, for an everyday hero like you, it's important to be ready when the save-the-day siren sounds.

Every home should have at least one fire extinguisher, and when you go shopping for one, look for the codes on the canisters, which should be by the fine print on the label. If you see *A*, that means the extinguisher works best on combustibles like wood, paper, and cloth, while *B* is best for flammable liquids, and *C* works well for live electricity. Another part of the code to keep in mind is the numbers before the letters. So you might see something like 2-A or 4-B. Those numbers indicate how effective the extinguisher will be with each type of fire, and the higher the number the better it will work. So you'd want a 4-A over a 1-A, for example. Knowing those letters will help you make the best choice while buying.

Now to actually save the day and extinguish a fire, all you need to remember is the PASS acronym. (Are you getting some flashbacks from a very special lesson in middle school about how to work an extinguisher?)

PASS outlines exactly what to do when faced with unwanted flames: pull, aim, squeeze, and sweep. The first part of PASS, the **P**, stands for pulling the safety pin from the fire extinguisher handle. **A** means you should aim the nozzle or hose at the base of the fire, and not at the flames. Then you **S**, squeeze the handle slowly to discharge the carbon dioxide. The last **S** stands for the sweeping side-to-side motion you'll make with the hose or nozzle until the flames are extinguished. The next invisible **S** stands for superhero, which is exactly what you'll be.

7 MAKE YOUR OWN ALL-PURPOSE CLEANING SOLUTION

What doesn't kill you only makes you stronger—and some of it will hopefully kill the germs in your kitchen as well. That's right: with an all-purpose DIY cleaner, you can bet that those germs won't be sticking around for long.

So when you need to clean house, just grab water, white vinegar, and a few drops of an essential oil—lemon, tea tree, or lavender, for example. You're probably thinking, *But wait, that's only three things, how does that work?* Here's the deal: The acid in white vinegar helps to dissolve grease and soap scum, while the essential oil will provide a pleasant smell along with some antifungal qualities. Combine those two and you've got a winning combo for cleanliness.

To actually make the cleaning solution, combine one part water, one part vinegar, and a few drops of the essential oil. Shake it all up and use it in a spray bottle or pour it out onto a cloth. If you're feeling super ambitious, do both of these things. Remember that it won't kill you, but it will kill the germs.

8 REMOVE RUG AND CARPET STAINS

Rugs are the true heartbreakers of the décor world, because no matter how hard you try to keep them clean, they will get dirty. Someone will spill wine, you'll track in dirt, or the universe will deliver the dreaded mystery stain—you won't know where it came from, but it will be there to taunt you.

But take heart, because you can combat the universe and that mystery stain pretty easily. For smaller spot treatments, start by pouring a little vinegar over the stain—just enough to soak it. Then sprinkle baking soda over the vinegar and let it sit and bubble so it can absorb the stain. After a few minutes, take a damp cloth and run it over the spot. Voilà, it's gone!

If it's something a little trickier—say, red wine or the leftovers from last night's greasy takeout—you'll want to go the extra mile. Mix Dawn dishwashing liquid soap with a little hydrogen peroxide and pour it on your stain. Once it's soaked for a few minutes, scrub at the stain with a cloth until it's all been lifted.

9   GET RID OF FRUIT FLIES

Fruit flies are like houseguests who just won't leave. They're also annoyingly ambitious, as they can lay up to five hundred eggs near ripening fruit, and often will go above and beyond by laying eggs in sink drains, garbage

disposals, trashcans, and even wet sponges. All they want to do is hang, while all you can think about is leaving immediately.

As soon as you see those familiar flies zip around the kitchen, the first thing you need to do is make sure they can't lay their eggs anywhere. This means it's time to put all fruits and veggies in the fridge and make sure there aren't any remnants of food in the disposal or trashcans.

From there, you're going to put on your tough-as-nails face and prepare for battle. You have two main options at this point. You can buy a disposable fruit fly trap from your local hardware store, or get going on your next DIY project.

One DIY option is to take a jar and put a piece of ripened fruit inside. That's going to serve as your bait. But in order to nab the flies, you're going to create a trap. To do that, you'll take a piece of paper and roll it into a cone. You'll then put the top of the cone (the narrowest part) into the jar, so that when fruit flies race in to get the fruit, they aren't able to fly back out easily.

Another way to end the fruit fly madness is to grab a jar and fill it one-fourth full with beer, wine, or apple cider vinegar, all of which are very enticing to a fruit fly. You'll then cover the jar with plastic wrap, and poke a few holes that are big enough for a fly to get in, but small enough for them to have a hard time flying out. Just act fast so your unwelcome houseguest doesn't move the whole family in as well.

10 CLEAN YOUR KITCHEN SPONGES

Ten minutes spent worrying about the last time you changed out the sponge is ten minutes when you could've been doing something infinitely better (searching the internet for photos of cats, for example). This is why

knowing how to properly clean your sponges, and when to send them to sponge heaven, will ensure you never waste precious minutes again.

It's probably no surprise that sponges are carriers of bacteria. After all, you use them to clean, wipe, and absorb. Since they're in such heavy rotation, it's important that every time they do those things, they aren't spreading germs onto new surfaces.

To keep sponges clean and safe, disinfect them weekly. Soaking a sponge for five minutes in a solution of 3 tablespoons of bleach to 4 cups of water will do the trick. If your sponge is metal-free, you can also soak it in water, then zap it in the microwave for two minutes. The heat will nuke the bacteria. Just make sure to give it time to cool down before grabbing it!

When should you stop trying to save a sponge and send it on its way to sponge heaven? If a sponge starts to smell, that's generally a good time to throw it in the trash. Also, should you use a sponge to clean up any meat juices—poultry or beef, for example—then it should be tossed. In general, if you're using your sponge regularly, you should replace it at least once a month.

11 KNOW WHEN TO WASH YOUR TOWELS AND SHEETS

It really is the little things in life that make all the difference. After a long day, there's nothing quite as satisfying as cuddling up in your clean, warm sheets and falling fast asleep.

What you might not be thinking about while you're dozing off is that if you want to stay clean, you should be washing your sheets around once a week. Because if you think about it, every time you sleep in them, those sheets are building up sweat, debris, hair, and dust, among other things. Which is why you have to change and wash them weekly. If that seems fairly frequent, just remember that you don't want your cuddle time to be interrupted by germs.

Bath towels have an even shorter lifespan. This one might surprise you, because they should be washed after just three uses. Yup, three! That's because not only does the towel stay damp for a while after use, accumulating mold and bacteria, but each time you pat yourself dry, that towel's also absorbing all of your dead skin cells. Gross. So, yeah, third time's the charm for towels.

But the shortest shelf life of all is for kitchen towels. Every time you're drying a plate, wiping your hands off, or using it to handle food, that rag is attracting all kinds of bacteria and germs. So experts say you should wash a kitchen towel after each use by tossing it in the laundry.

Just remember that these little rules for washing will make your everyday life a whole lot more sanitary!

12   REMOVE PET HAIR FROM ANY SURFACE

Ah, pet hair: cute on your furry friend, and not so cute on your couch. Unfortunately, cleaning up your pet's fur isn't always as simple as using a vacuum or going over an area with a lint roller.

For any furniture that your bestie has been happily rolling around on, try using a rubber glove to get the fur up. All you need to do is put the rubber glove on and gently rub the surface of the furniture with it. This may seem (and look) weird, but it really works. You'll start to see the fur come up in clumps, and when the glove gets too fuzzy you can wash it in the sink, so long as it has a trap in the drain to prevent hair clogs. Any excess fur you dislodge can then be easily removed with a vacuum or lint roller.

If your pet is more interested in shedding on the carpet or rug, you can rub a pumice stone gently across the surface to lift the pet hair up. But if you're trying to clean hardwood, laminate, or other bare floors, use an electrostatic or microfiber mop to bring up the hair. You'll be amazed at how much cuter your home looks when it isn't growing a fur coat of its own.

13 HANG CURTAINS

If done correctly, your curtains can make your home look *très* chic, but if a little too much is taken off the bottom it'll make your home look *très* cheap. So read up on these tips and tricks before you hang those curtains.

One of the easiest rules is that the longer they are, the better, because curtains work as visual cues in a room. So the closer you hang your curtains to the ceiling, the more that vertical curtain line will draw the eye up, creating the illusion of height even if you live in a Hobbit hole. With

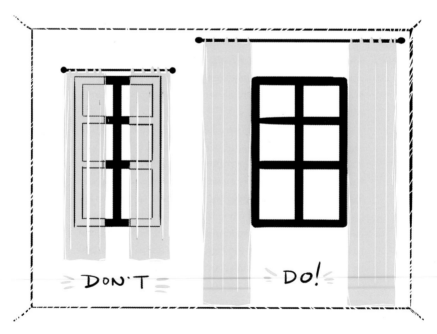

that vertical line, you want your curtains to hit the ceiling and also fall to the floor—the longer the line, the taller the room looks. The curtains can float slightly above the floor, but if you go too short, you're wandering dangerously close to that *très* cheap territory.

To get that initial length part right, you'll want to measure your space before you buy. Use a tape measure to get the height of the wall and the width of the window. You'll want to look for curtains that are tall enough to be mounted close to the ceiling and just hit the floor, and wide enough to cover two times the width of the window, ideally.

Next, pick a rod—you'll likely see a classic rod, return rod, or tension rod. Valance curtains can be hung on a classic or return rod, while grommet, tab top, and café curtains can be hung on any rod. It's all about preference. If you can't drill into your walls, or simply don't want to, another option are the adhesive hooks, which act as no-drill curtain rod holders.

Once you've got the curtains and rod, it's time to get on the ladder. You'll want to place your rod about two to four inches below the ceiling to enhance the illusion of height. You can mark where to place the curtain rod bracket (the thing you'll drill into the wall) with a pencil and a level. Just make sure the bracket is a few inches wider than the actual window so your curtains cover the whole window.

Honestly, drilling in your brackets is the hardest part, aside from picking a curtain color, and that's mainly because you have to stand on a ladder. But once they're drilled in, you're about to cross the finish line. Simply insert the rod through the holes or ties of the curtains, and you're ready to go. Just lift the rod, place it on the brackets, and you'll have your own *très* chic window dressing.

A change of paint can do you good. Especially if you reward yourself with a much-deserved beer after completing the paint job.

Before you start, though, it's important to prep, because (if you didn't already learn this in kindergarten) paint is messy. Unless you want your stuffed toy from childhood splattered in venetian blue, remove loose items you love from the floor, and cover any remaining furniture with a sheet. Tape the corners and edges of your walls that you don't want covered in paint, like the ceiling or the molding, and secure a drop cloth to the floor. Sensing a pattern here? Yeah, essentially you want to keep the paint where it's supposed to be and prevent it from jumping ship onto your hardwood.

Once you've prepped, it's time for the fun part: painting like a pro. Try to buy a paint and primer in one, but if you need to paint over dark colors, use a primer first. If you have any trouble popping open the paint can, use a screwdriver to nudge the lip of the can open. Then pour your paint into a tray so you can dip your brushes and rollers with ease.

To save yourself a headache, start by painting the corners of the walls with a small paintbrush. Getting those outer edges, which tend to be the most time consuming, out of the way first will ensure that you can speed your way through the rest. Once the outer edges are done, go across the wall with your bigger roller brush. To avoid any roller marks, paint in an *M* motion. Once the entire wall is coated, step back and evaluate whether it needs another coat. If you're totally done, pop open a beer—you and those painting arms have earned it.

15   FIND A STUD IN THE WALL

A good stud is hard to find. Not *that* kind of stud, but the studs in the framework of your home (AKA the vertical pieces of wood that help hold the walls up). That wood, when found, can serve as an anchor for whatever you want to nail to the wall.

Small items can be hung on most walls without a hitch, but if you're veering into the ten-to-fifteen-pounds category, then you'll want to find that stud in the wall. So whether you're nailing up a framed piece of art, a TV mount, or a giant mirror, you can walk into a room with your hammer held high because *you* know how to find the stud.

And knowing where one stud is can help you find the next one. To locate a stud, start from the edge of an electrical unit or corner of a room and measure in sixteen-inch

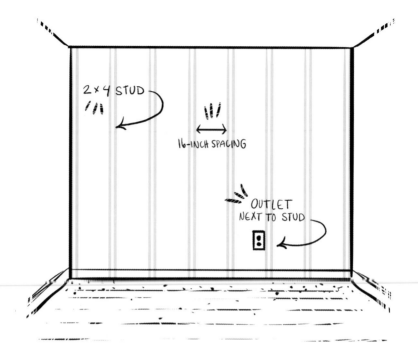

intervals horizontally, as building codes in most contemporary homes require they be placed at least sixteen inches apart on center. Once you measure sixteen inches out from the first stud, you'll have the next one, and so on.

Or if you have a strong magnet in your house, you can use that. Tie the magnet to a piece of floss or string, and slowly go horizontally across the walls with it. When the magnet hits a stud, which should be filled with nails from the wood plank nailed to it, the magnet will pull a bit more. You have to go slowly along the wall, but this totally works. Hey, finding the right stud takes time.

16 KEEP YOUR PLANTS ALIVE

How many of your tchotchkes can create ambiance, reduce stress levels, *and* purify the air? None is the answer. That's why houseplants are the most valuable players in home décor. Yet it can be hard to keep house-plants from the edge of demise.

Let's start at the beginning. There are a few things to keep in mind when you bring new plants into your home, like how often to water them. In general, when their soil is slightly dry to the touch, you can feel free to add more H_2O, but doing a quick Google search on your new friend is always a smart idea. The typical indoor houseplants also need to get the right amount of sun, but they actually don't need *that* much sunlight every day, and putting plants in a spot that's overly sunny can kill them as well. Aim for a location that isn't in direct sunlight and doesn't get overly hot. At this point it might seem like plants are high-maintenance, but they just have high standards—hence that MVP title!

Spritzing a plant's leaves with a little water every so often—as those can get dry too—will also keep it happy. And speaking of being too dry, put your plant on top of pebbles in a shallow tray with water to make sure your friend is getting the humidity it needs to thrive.

With thriving comes growth, and some spreading roots, so once a year lift your plant out of its pot and check the roots—do they seem tightly wound together? Then the plant needs a bigger pot home. If not, the plant can happily stay where it is and keep that MVP title.

17 STYLE YOUR SOFA

For something you sit on, couches sure can make a big impact in a room—and they sure can cost a lot of money too. Before you spring for a new sofa that eats an entire paycheck, though, consider treating your current sofa to some stylish threads.

If your sofa is a neutral shade, then opting for a pop of color with a throw pillow or blanket can brighten up the

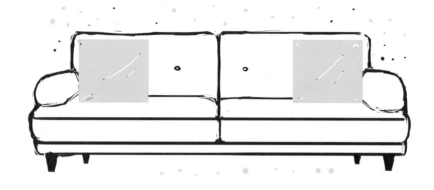

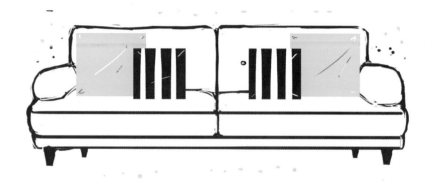

whole room. That accent piece can be a solid or a cool printed pattern, and if you're in a mix-and-match mood, then you can do both so long as they're complementary colors. On the opposite end of the spectrum, if you have a brightly colored couch, like a yellow, a neutral throw color, like gray, can be a nice complement.

In terms of how many throw pillows to add—after all, you want to make sure there's enough room for you to curl up on your couch—the easiest option would be two accent pillows, with at least twenty-four inches of height each. If you want to layer a few pillows, then keep the bigger throw pillows in the back and put the smaller ones toward the front. That will ensure that each pillow gets its proper amount of exposure without a cluttered look.

18   ADD LINER TO YOUR DRAWERS

So you've realized that your drawer has become a bottomless pit of old ticket stubs and bills, and you want to spruce it up before a swamp creature moves in. Not to fear; drawer liners are here to turn your drawer into something worth opening (no swamp creatures allowed)!

If you're aiming for simplicity, buy adhesive drawer liner from a home goods store. Then measure the inside of the drawer, cut the contact paper to fit that size, remove the adhesive backing, and apply it to the bottom of the drawer. It's a quick and easy way to get beautifully lined drawers.

But making a DIY drawer liner is just as painless and allows you to pick whatever pattern you like. If you want to line your dresser drawers, buy fabric so your clothing has something soft to sit on. If you're lining the drawers in a bathroom or kitchen, stick with paper to avoid any mold. You can go to a craft store to buy a paper pattern, or even use old maps or pages from your favorite books.

Regardless of your material, start by measuring the width and length of the drawer, and cut out the fabric or paper with about an extra inch tacked on to the length you measured. That extra inch will provide some cushion so you don't fall short in the end. Then you'll want to fit the paper or fabric into the drawer. Once it's in, fold the excess material (that extra inch or so) over and make a clear crease. When you remove the material from the drawer, you'll cut the excess off at the crease with a craft knife or scissors.

Now that you've got the liner ready to go, it's time to secure it to the drawer. Use double-sided tape or a spray adhesive and carefully insert your liner in the drawer. The next time you open it up, that bottomless pit will, at the very least, be a much fancier one.

Comfortable, welcoming, and *ample* are all words to get behind when describing your space. But if you're dealing with a small room or you pick the wrong furniture, you may have to face the fact that the words *cramped, claustrophobic*, and *uncomfortable* are more accurate.

Let's avoid those latter words. Whether you're short on space or just want tips to make any room appear more grandiose than it really is, there are ways to make your vision a reality.

Making a room feel tall and airy is the goal here. So utilize visual tricks, like painting the ceiling, to draw the eyes up and add height. Similarly, a striped rug can make it feel as if there's more length to a room. You can also make use of vertical lines with a tall bookshelf, curtains that start at the ceiling and fall to the ground, or shelves near the ceiling. Those will all draw the eye up and make it feel as if your space is much larger than it is.

To get that airy feel, you'll need to lighten the room. Do that by keeping the walls and floors a light color. Also opt for sleek and uncluttered furniture to allow breathing room in your home. Similarly, make sure that your furniture isn't pressed up against a wall by leaving a little room behind it. This will produce the illusion that there's space (even if there isn't).

One of the simplest ways to make a room seem larger is just to lean or hang a long mirror against a wall. The mirror will help to reflect light and create a sense of movement in a space, effectively banning the word *cramped* forever.

romantic prowess

THIS MAY COME AS A COLOSSAL SHOCK (read: not a shock at all), but sex, dating, and love are really important parts of everyone's life. Even if you've never experienced any of them, it's still all around you and unavoidable. Romance is on the TV shows you watch, it's what your friends often vent about, and for better or worse it's what we spend a lot of our own time mulling over.

Romance is more than just a candlelit dinner and staring longingly into another person's beautiful eyes, if you're into that kind of thing. Now more than ever, women have a much bigger say in how things go. We can ask someone out on a date or even ask someone for their hand in marriage. You can be single for the rest of your life if you want or be a woman who knows what she wants and isn't afraid to ask for it in bed. Choice is the big thing here, and you get to make your own choices about what kind of a romantic life you want to have.

This chapter isn't just a reminder that as a woman you have the power to dictate what you want romantically. It will also cover so many stages of your love life—from navigating a first date to knowing when to say yes to moving in. You don't have to be a helpless romantic to have a successful relationship, and you don't have to feel bad if the idea of a relationship seriously isn't your thing. It's all about figuring out what you want when it comes to your love life, and this chapter will hopefully help you do just that.

1 BE HAPPY BEING SINGLE

Being single means you've been given the gift of time to figure out what you need to be content. In the words of RuPaul, "If you can't love yourself, how the hell you gonna love somebody else?"

If you don't know where to start, try doing things you know will relax you—going for a long walk, checking out a new art exhibit, getting a massage, reading a book—whatever it is, do it. The idea is to get you to a place where being alone isn't a burden; it's fun.

Once you're able to associate alone time with positive feelings, then start getting out of your daily routine and challenging yourself to take on new adventures. Maybe you've always wanted to learn how to surf, or maybe you've wanted to take a trip to visit your college friends. Explore the options you previously haven't, and make time for the things that interest you. By doing these things, you'll become more confident in yourself and get closer to feeling fulfilled on your own without the help of a significant other.

If bettering yourself means discovering new activities you love, then it's also about finding new health and body goals. Eliminate the bad habits you've been holding onto so you can move forward into healthier ones. Drink for fun and not to excess. Start a new exercise regime that makes you feel empowered. And really look at your diet

to assess whether or not what you're eating is helping or hurting you. Eating poorly can often affect happiness, so consider how far you're willing to go to change your habits for the better.

When you're content with where you are in life, other people will pick up on that and want to be around you. You know, sexy people whom you can potentially have sexy times with. So make time for yourself, and the rest will fall into place.

2   ASK SOMEONE ON A DATE

There are three important *be*'s to being a woman: be bold, be brave, and be confident enough to ask someone on a date. Think about it. The worst thing that can happen is they say no, but the best-case scenario is that you've got a date with someone worthy of your time.

An easy step toward a happy first date is to make sure the person you're asking is single and ready to mingle. This one will be a nonissue if you're meeting people on a dating app, as they're obviously looking, but if it's in real life, try to do some sleuthing through conversations—or even some good old-fashioned internet searches. In the spirit of directness, a simple, "So, are you seeing anyone?" will do the trick.

If you know you're going to ask someone out ahead of time, try to wear something that makes you feel poised and fearless. Or call your bestie for a pep talk beforehand. Do whatever you need to build up your courage.

Now, for the actual asking—the part where all of your nerves bundle up to try and work against you. It's best to be specific about the fact that this is a date, and you're interested in the person. So avoid saying things like "Do

GREAT WAYS TO ASK SOMEONE ON A DATE

"You seem like a person who would appreciate mac and cheese; should we go eat some together?"

"I just realized we've never gone bowling together before. Should we do that this weekend?"

"If you go hiking with me sometime, I promise to bring a snack pack in case we get lost."

"I'd put you in my top ten conversationalists ever. So, can we get dinner this weekend and continue conversing?"

"I have a feeling you've got at least one weird story from high school—wanna go get a drink so I can find out if I'm right?"

you want to hang out sometime?" in favor of "Would you want to get dinner on Saturday?" Be honest so there's no confusion about what you're after.

If they give you a flat-out no, then it's game over. This person clearly isn't worth additional time; reboot with someone else. But if the person simply is busy that night, it could mean that there's some interest. So be ready to come back with some alternate dates and see what happens. Chances are you'll be able to find an option that works for both of you. If the person is indefinitely busy, however, that's your cue to move on.

Regardless of the answer you get, you're a bold, brave woman who's confident enough to ask someone else out. And that's the most important thing.

3 NAVIGATE THE FIRST-DATE CONVERSATION

Here's a riddle: What has two people, four sweaty palms, and a lot of awkward small talk? That's right, it's the first-date conversation! But with a few tricks, you can take that first-date convo from an awkward place to a fun one.

Take initiative and ask questions so you're not waiting for your date to get the conversation going. Things such as "What's the best meal you've ever had?" "How many siblings do you have?" and "Where's your favorite place to go in the city?" are all great options.

Which leads to the next meaningful conversation factor: listening. On first dates it's easy to get nervous and overtalk, or start thinking of the next thing to ask before the person has finished speaking. But listening will help both of you feel at ease and allow you both to find those first-date questions more naturally.

And when it comes to questions, a first date isn't the time to dig into someone's dark past. In other words, if you're happily talking about where you grew up, the next logical question isn't, "So what happened with all of your exes?" There's no need to bring up the super heavy stuff on a first date—you're just getting to know each other, and this should be fun, not emotionally draining for both of you.

Similarly, a first date isn't an opportune time to have a therapy session. This person doesn't need to know that the last person you dated moved out because you both cheated and admitted it while on Thanksgiving vacations with your families. For a first date, try to leave your baggage at home where it belongs—you can bring it out later when you know each other better.

4   LET SOMEONE DOWN EASY

Who ya gonna call? Not Ghostbusters, because you are not going to ghost someone. You know, ghosting, the thing where instead of telling someone how you really feel, you simply vanish altogether. The cycle of ghosting ends here, and the journey to giving people closure begins (because you'd want the same thing).

It's perfectly fine to not want to go on a first date with someone or to not want to see someone again. So now that that's out of the way, it's on to how to end things. If you've been dating for less than a month and you haven't gotten super serious, a text is totally fine. Here are some acceptable options you can choose from:

For the person who asked you out, but you're not interested: "I think you're such a fantastic person, but I just don't see you that way."

For the person you went on one date with: "Hey, it was great meeting you, but I don't see this going anywhere. All the best!"

For someone you've been on one to three dates with: "It's been so cool getting to know you, but I don't see this

going anywhere and I wanted to be honest, since I respect you. Hope you meet someone wonderful."

When the person seems super into you, but you're not vibing: "Sorry to text you this, as I've had a really amazing time with you, but I'm just not ready to date right now. Thought I was, but I realized I'm not. It was great getting to know you though."

If these texts feel too simplistic or if you've been dating longer than a month, then you likely need an in-person meeting or a phone call, as more explanation is called for. Remember to be direct, make things clear and final, and treat the person the way you'd want to be treated if the tables were turned.

5   FIGHT FAIR

Pat Benatar was wrong. Love doesn't have to be a battle-field. With the right tools, every time you go to war over something, so to speak, you can do so with the goal of peace and happily-ever-afters in mind.

Just know that as a human being, you will have times when you'll be annoyed or frustrated at another person. This is totally normal, and when you feel upset, you should air your grievances right away instead of holding on to them. When you hold your feelings in, it just leads to a bigger and more complicated argument.

And because you're a fair fighter, you should always be willing to negotiate. In other words, no one will "win" this fight. You're both going to enter into it with the understanding that something is wrong, and you need to fix it. There's no sense in trying to win a fight; just hear the other person out and come to a consensus.

If you do have to fight, be understanding of the other person's time and space. If either of you is exhausted, that isn't the right time. If you're in your office or your partner's—a location that isn't neutral—that isn't the place to do it. Find a neutral location, and choose a time when you both can be fully present to fight fair.

And above all, avoid saying mean, hateful things about your partner's character. Don't play the blame game, and don't call each other names that you won't be able to take back. Once you start with the name-calling, the only thing your partner can do in response is to call you a name back. Names stick in the memory, so avoid them at all costs. If you do, you're more likely to have a productive discussion than an all-out battle.

The difference between being in a relationship and just being friends is—drum roll please—the sex. So figuring out how to make that sex satisfying, which can often include some constructive feedback, is crucial.

When you want to give pointers to a partner, it's best to start with the positive. If your partner does something you like (even if only for a minute), make sure you say so. Either in the moment or after you're finished, you can bring it up by saying something like "I really loved that thing you did when you (insert awesome thing here). More of that, please!" Or if your partner got close to doing what you wanted, say that too. "I really loved when you did this thing; next time could you try doing this other thing?"

If the problem is something that needs more direction—like more foreplay, or maybe you really prefer having sex in the morning—then wait to talk about it when your partner is feeling comfortable and not vulnerable (not necessarily while naked in your bed). You can start the conversation with something along the lines of "I really love it when we have morning sex; I just seem to climax more often."

Another way to approach the issue is through a "we" stance rather than a "you" one. So saying, "Why don't we play a game where we can only have foreplay for the next half hour," is going to be smoother than, "You don't spend enough time on me before we have sex." The goal is not to blame the other person but to open up a conversation so you both end up having more fun.

When life gives you a miserable relationship, make the choice to not be miserable. Breaking up is hard to do, but instead of wasting another minute of your time and your partner's, own the fact that it isn't working and do something about it.

The first step is realizing that your relationship isn't working, which can be a really tough thing to admit. Thinking about exactly why it isn't working for you is necessary, because you should be prepared to explain those reasons to the other person.

It may be tempting to end things by simply running as fast as you can away from the person. But you're a strong, independent woman, so you're not going to run from your problems. Instead, you're going to pick a thoughtful time and place to have this incredibly difficult conversation. Remember that while this conversation is difficult for you, it's going to be even more emotional for them. Because while you've had time to accept that you're about to break up, they're only just hearing about it. So keep that in mind before deciding on a location and time.

Since you're the one doing the dumping, it's essential to be honest about why the relationship isn't working, and avoid placing all the blame on the other person. A breakup stings enough without hearing that you're the worst (even if you are). Things like "We fight all the time" are going to hurt less than "You're always fighting me over petty stuff." And because you have the high ground in this situation, keep in mind that the person may be extremely upset. So be sympathetic in the moment, even if you can't wait to get out of there.

If, for whatever reason, your partner can't seem to let things go, or if you've been dating for a very long time, you can suggest taking a break to ease into the breakup. It will give that person time to accept that things aren't going well, and when you reconvene, just reiterate what you've already said. Breaking up is hard to do, so giving the other person the time and respect they deserve will ease their pain and yours.

8 HANDLE AN EX

The ball is truly in your court when it comes to how to handle an ex. You can try to stay friends, or be friendly acquaintances, or erase the person from your life altogether. But if you plan to stay on good terms, which can be complicated, there are some ways to do just that.

Start by setting boundaries—not just for the ex, but for yourself and any new significant other. Those boundaries might mean that you need to give each other a proper cooling-off period so you have time to mourn and move past the relationship. Or that in order to hang out, you need to avoid places where both of you have strong memories. These boundaries are meant to help you decide what's OK versus not OK in this new friendship, and you may have to use some trial and error to get to solid ground.

In the spirit of trial and error, don't forget to be patient with an ex. It will take a significant amount of time for both of you to figure out how to behave and treat each other, so allow for that. And don't badmouth your ex, especially when you have mutual friends. This separation isn't just hard for you two, it's hard for your friends, and forcing them to choose sides or hear your dirty laundry puts them in a really tough position.

If it gets to a point where your ex isn't respecting the boundaries you've put in place or is having trouble distinguishing that friend-girlfriend line, then consider cutting ties permanently. If you've restated the boundaries and have been considerate of your ex's feelings but your ex is still not respecting yours, then ceasing contact is the best option. Just remember that the ball is in your court, and it's up to you if you want to play.

9   MEET THE PARENTS FOR THE FIRST TIME

Meeting the parents is so stressful, there's already a three-movie series about it. Hopefully when you meet your SO's parents, it won't be fodder for a fourth movie.

To get this important meeting off on the right foot, start by dressing the part. Of course what matters is on the inside, but since your physical appearance is the first thing the parents will see, it's wise not to overlook it. Err on the side of caution, meaning you should almost dress as if you're going for a job interview. You don't want anything too flashy or distracting, as you want them to see you and not be distracted by your sequined vest. And remember to load on the deodorant, because chances are you'll be doing some sweating.

If you're meeting the parents for the first time and staying with them in their house, a nice touch is to get a gift to thank them for their hospitality. Ask your significant other about the parents' likes or dislikes and go from there.

And you should prepare for typical questions your own parents would ask: How did you two meet? What's your current job like? What do you want to be doing in the future? Similarly, ask your significant other if there are topics you shouldn't bring up—maybe they have different political ideas than you do, for example. Either way, getting the prep work done ahead of time will calm your nerves.

Speaking of nerves, remember to pace yourself if there's any drinking involved. Even if the family is hugely into partying, you'll want to watch how much you drink the first time you're meeting them. The last thing you want to do is wake up in the morning next to a toilet.

In general, though, the main thing about parents is that they just want to know you make their kid happy. So the safest and easiest way to get on their good side is to gush about your significant other. The more gushing, the more likely they are to gush about you when you leave.

10 MEET THE FRIENDS FOR THE FIRST TIME

Meeting a partner's friends should be a piece of cake. And often, it *is* a piece of cake—just one topped with a dollop of anxiety. That's because unlike meeting the parents, you'll have to interact with your partner's friends on a regular basis. Which means you'll really have to work hard to win them over.

If you don't know anything about the friends, ask your significant other for intel—their names, where they met your SO, what they like—to get a sense of the types of people they are. Having that knowledge will also put you at ease since you won't be entering into the conversations totally blind.

If you're meeting a larger group, you'll be able to spot a friendlier face out of the bunch. That's the one asking you questions or making an effort to say hello. This is the person you should strike up a conversation with first. Since they're already game to give you precious minutes of their time, talking to them will warm you up and will give others a chance to hop into a larger conversation as well.

If you're hanging with just one to two friends, a good rule of thumb is to ask plenty of questions, listen to the answers, and have some follow-up questions ready. It takes the pressure off of you and allows time to hear what they're into.

In general, the main thing with friends is they want to know whether or not you can hang out with them. In a way, they're just making sure you're "cool." So when in doubt, or if you're feeling nervous, let your partner lead the conversations. After all, they're not your friends . . . yet.

11 MOVE IN TOGETHER

The Big Move, which is a fair thing to call moving in together, is a life-changing decision. Even if it seems simple in theory—box things up and move into a shared space, yay!—it's a huge step.

Think about a few things before the move, like how you feel when you spend a night apart. If you feel relieved to have some space, or look forward to it a little too much, you may need more time alone before moving in. But if you're already spending most nights together, that's a good indicator you're ready to move forward.

As you get ready for the Big Move, you'll want to sort out some of the finer details. Like, should you set up a joint account to cover expenses for rent and bills? How will you be divvying up the household chores? Just talking

about the details of this shift, big and small, will clear the air of any annoyances to come. Cleanliness can be a point of contention in relationships, so if you and your partner have different cleaning styles, discuss that and make sure you're on the same page—your partner won't be your maid and vice versa. You'll also want to talk about budget before any big move. What can you two afford? When it comes to groceries, will you both be paying an equal amount or finding another way to split those costs fairly? Budget talk isn't exactly sexy, but hammering out the details beforehand will save you some arguments later.

If you are totally sure this is the right move for you, then excellent! You will, of course, still need to decide if it's best to move into one of your current places or if you'd prefer to look for a new place together. Either choice has its perks and downsides, so just be clear in how you're feeling throughout the moving-in process.

Once you're living together, life will be wonderful in so many ways, but it's also a significant change. First and foremost, let certain things go. Maybe your partner constantly loads the toilet paper roll "wrong," or forgets to wash the dishes. You can absolutely discuss these things, but know when to pick your battles. It's also really crucial to make time for yourself and remember to have your own life outside of the house—don't become a hermit who disowns her friends the minute she makes the Big Move. And above all else, approach every situation with love—even if your partner makes you angry, remember that this is a person you adore and live with, and you need to act accordingly.

12 MAKE TIME FOR THE LITTLE THINGS

Upgrading your relationship doesn't mean you need to buy a soaking tub for two. That's because when it comes to a long-term relationship, it's the little things that will

end up mattering most. And doing small things each day is a lot easier than planning that picnic on top of a hot air balloon while a violinist plays "your" song. Just upgrade one little gesture at a time.

If you're not sure where to start, consider making a ritual out of something to help you remember to be thoughtful. Maybe it's waking up earlier than your significant other to deliver a cup of coffee or having a night each week when you cook dinner. Having a ritual, even though it may seem small, can make a huge difference in your relationship. When strung together each day, those little moments of thoughtfulness add up to a lot of positive memories for your partner.

Other ways to make time for the little things are to simply be more considerate of each other. Saying thank you more often and showing gratitude when your partner offers to help you makes a difference. And making an effort to incorporate more physical touching with each other—however small—will help to foster more intimacy. So go ahead: grab a hand or a butt cheek or plant a kiss each and every time your SO walks into a room. It'll be a fun way for you to add in some upgrades and also great for your long-term relationship.

13 PROPOSE MARRIAGE

Because of the patriarchy (shakes fist!), proposing has traditionally been the responsibility of a man in heterosexual relationships. But the future is here and now, and you definitely don't need to wait for anyone to propose, because you can do that all on your own.

If you want to propose, that means you're head-over-heels for someone—and that's super exciting. Take some time to think about that person and your future together. Do you have the same goals for your careers and financial

stability? How about when it comes to having children? And most importantly, does this person make you laugh? If the answers to these questions are yes, yes, and yes, then moving forward likely makes a lot of sense.

You also want to take into account your significant other's feelings—is there a chance they may not be ready for this or will feel hurt by not getting to propose? If it's a yes to either of those, then talking to your partner about your future together and bringing up these topics is a smart idea.

However, if you're sure this person is The One and that proposing is the next move to make, then it's time to get a ring. Do your research before shopping to see average prices and to find stores near you that might stock what you're looking for. If your partner is environmentally conscious, then search for a conflict-free stone, or opt for an antique piece of jewelry.

Timing and location are other big considerations to take into account. Would your SO want a proposal with friends and family present or something more intimate? Is there a date of significance coming up, like a favorite holiday or an anniversary, that you could use as a perfect way to propose?

With the ring and timing in mind, you've got the two most critical pieces in place. All you need to do now is ask and wait for your partner to say yes, making this one of the happiest days of your life. Congrats, you two!

14 PICK A WEDDING VENUE

In terms of the building blocks of a wedding, the venue is the foundation (literally and figuratively). Picking the venue is also a decision that will dictate the kind of wedding you'll have. So, in other words, this is big-deal stuff.

In order to pick a venue, you and your betrothed need to figure out the following: a guest list, so you can estimate how many people you want to invite; a budget you're comfortable with; and a time of year in which you'd ideally like to get married. You can have an idea of what you want, venue-wise, but it's also totally fine to not know that up front.

Research venues online, call them to make sure they're within your budget, and schedule appointments to tour the ones that appeal to you. When you go, have a long list of questions you'd like answers to, like "Do you provide tables and chairs?" "Can we bring our own booze to save money?" and "How late can the party run?" There are great sample questions on most wedding sites, which will guide you on how to find the right spot for your big day.

And while you may already know this, deciding on a venue will set the tone for your wedding. Hosting it in a backyard versus a formal ballroom, for example, means you have more wiggle room with your attire, the decorations, and even the food. So be mindful of what kind of a wedding you want before you sign on the dotted line. And a venue will also determine how much work you'll need to put into the wedding. For example, having a built-in caterer will be significantly less work than a venue where you have to hire an outside caterer to come in.

Just don't lose sight of the overall goal: to find a space where you can happily get married and where everyone can feel the specialness of the day.

ROMANTIC PROWESS

Here comes the bride . . . and all of the people who so gra-
ciously agreed to fork over a significant amount of money
to be part of your bridal party. Yes, this is your special day,
but your wedding is not just about you. (Sorry!) So when
you're picking the members of your bridal party, know
that while you're doing something incredibly thoughtful,
this is also a massive commitment for them.

Make a list of everyone you'd ideally want to be part
of your bridal party. Do it with reckless abandon and the
kind of idealism that's usually reserved for hopeful college freshmen. Once you have that list, take a good hard
look at it. Is it absurdly long? Do some people on the list
hate each other? Do you secretly hate some of them? As
you trim that list down, you want to think about how your
bridesmaids and bridesmen will feel when they're trapped
in a room together. If you know some of them won't get
along, consider careful trimming. If you know that fifteen
people is about ten people too many, start cutting.

Other things to keep in mind are that you don't have to include people just because you were in their wedding party. If you think they can't handle the financial strain of being part of a bridal party (which can cost thousands of dollars), offer the option to decline.

When you've considered all of these factors, it's finally time to think about you. Will you be friends with these people in the long term? Are they prone to being wildly inappropriate or taking actions that could potentially dampen your wedding? And do they have your best interests at heart? Even though being part of a bridal party is super fun, it's also a lot of work—someone has to hold the train, and wrangle the guests, and hold your dress while you use the bathroom (gross, but often true). So make sure the support team you're building in your bridal party is one you're totally confident in who will make your day blissful instead of stressful.

16 BE A MAID OF HONOR

Fasten your seat belts, because being a maid of honor is going to be a bumpy ride. Yes, to be asked is an amazing gift and gesture. Someone loves you so much that she's willing to put you near the center of wedding photos she'll look at for the rest of her life. That's incredible! Then you realize just how much work you have to do to honor this responsibility.

If you're excited for the bride, then you're already winning. There will be a lot of little moments your friend wants to celebrate, so making sure to indulge her in those is half the battle. OK, so maybe you don't care that her colors are ivory and lavender, but playing along will let the bride know you're there for her, even if you'd rather be doing anything else.

Just a few of the things you'll be in charge of leading up to the wedding are organizing a bachelorette party, hosting or cohosting a bridal shower, and making sure that your fellow bridesmaids are in the loop with picking out their dresses. You're basically assuming the role of a part-time event planner, which you can totally* add to your resume after the fact. (*Probably.)

Of course your most important duties will come on the day of the wedding. In a lot of ways you'll be fulfilling multiple roles: best friend, personal assistant, chef, damage controller, dress fixer, and emotions checker. As the best friend, you'll need to prepare a speech and give your friend all of the emotional support you can. As a personal assistant, you'll check in with the bride to make sure things like tips, transportation, and timing are taken care of. As the chef, you'll be feeding the bride throughout the day to ensure she doesn't pass out. You'll cover any damage control if something goes awry. When she walks down the aisle, as the dress fixer you'll adjust the train, veil, or any other little thing that you can. And as the emotions checker, you'll remind your friend that this is one of the happiest days of her life, because the last thing she wants to remember when she looks back is how stressed she was.

There's no doubt that the road to the wedding will have its bumps, but you'll be there making sure everyone's seat belt is fastened.

17 PICK YOUR PERFECT DRESS

Plenty of TV shows will lead you to believe that when you find *the* dress, the heavens will open, rays of glitter will pour down, and you'll burst into tears. But here's a reality check for those reality TV shows: that's not always the case.

To help you find a dress (or pantsuit, if you want) for your big day, there are a few insider tips to keep in mind, starting with your appointment. Make it in advance and

for first thing in the morning, because the salon will be less crowded and you'll have a consultant who's fresh and wanting to start the day with a sale. Meaning they'll work harder than someone at the end of the day who just wants to leave.

When describing your style to a salesperson, think about what is usually best on your body type. If you don't know, have that discussion with your consultant: "I'm on the shorter side, so what would you suggest?" And while a lot of brides focus on the train of a dress, you also really want to look at what a dress is offering from the waist up—as that's what will most often appear and be the focal point in photos. And finally, take into account what your betrothed would like, as this is not just your big day.

For the actual visit to the salon, instead of bringing everyone, just bring a close inner circle whom you deeply trust and love. If you have a friend who's a hater, leave that person at home. Bring people who will be honest without ruining this day in the process. One to three people is ideal, because as you increase the number, you increase your chances of being told conflicting opinions. And when you put the dress on, make sure to stand, sit, dance, and walk in it—you don't want to get to your wedding day and realize that your corset prevents you from bending at any point during the party.

Just don't feel bad if you don't cry when you find your wedding dress or if you don't have a "This is it!" moment. Some things, like avalanches of tears, are only made for TV.

18 GET GREAT WEDDING PHOTOS

If a picture is worth a thousand words, then a wedding photo is probably worth a million. While you'll take thousands of photos in your life, there usually aren't many days that will top your wedding day. So whether you're hiring a photographer or giving your nearest and dearest disposable cameras, knowing some tricks will ensure you have a picture-perfect day.

This may seem obvious, but whoever is taking photos won't know who's really important to you at your wedding. While you likely want photos with everyone, there might be that one uncle who traveled across the country and is really special to you. So make a list of people you'd like photos with, and feel free to give that to your photographer on the day of. It'll help for them to have a checklist, and for you to not stress out about forgetting to snap a pic with your favorite person.

Another thing to keep in mind is that a photographer

will be taking photos of you almost the entire day. So small details, like the fact that you're drinking out of a water bottle, can be eliminated if you think ahead and use nice glassware instead. Just remember that a lot of moments will be captured that day, so if there's something you'd rather not have in your shots (like all of your attendants' bags on a bed), make sure they're taken care of.

While traditional family portraits can be a pain—let's face it, you probably just want to get back to the wedding—they are important. Those are the photos your families will likely want framed, so have a list of people you need photos with, and grin until they're over. Yes, there's an actual celebration to get back to, but this is also a moment when you can capture lifelong memories.

And in terms of the actual photos, when posing try to get unnaturally close to your partner, as any gaps or spaces will be caught by the camera. If you're feeling tense or wound up, roll out your shoulders a few times before a photo so you'll look more relaxed. When in doubt, just smile—your happy face is what it's all about.

19 TIP YOUR VENDORS

As the saying goes, it takes a village. To pull off a great wedding, one of the biggest events of your life, you'll definitely need that village. And since that village will work hard to make your day special, you should repay the favor with a special tip.

Some vendors will include gratuity as part of your fee, which is lovely and makes your job significantly easier. But for those who don't, there are some things to know. First of all, most tips are given the day of the wedding. So to save you the stress of running around and tipping every waiter, assign that job to an attendant, family member, or your wedding coordinator.

If vendors own their own businesses, like florists, photographers, coordinators, or videographers, then tipping isn't expected. If they're employed by bigger companies,

HOW MUCH TO TIP

- **Wedding officiant:** Give a $75 to $100 donation to a charity. Tipping a wedding officiant or religious figure isn't expected, but if you want to give something, a donation in the person's name is generous.
- **Wedding planner:** Tip is optional and may be up to $500.
- **Hair and makeup artist:** Tip 15 to 25 percent.
- **Delivery and setup crew:** Tip $10. If someone delivers a big, important item, like your cake or flowers, slip the person a couple of bucks.
- **Catering staff:** Tip $20 for waiters, $50 for chefs, and $100 for the catering manager, only if gratuity isn't included in the bill.
- **Bartenders:** Tip $40 each.
- **Custodians:** Tip $25 each. A service fee may be included in your contract, but if it's not, you'll want to tip.
- **Musicians:** Tip is optional, but tip $25 per musician or $100 for a DJ.

then tipping fifty dollars is a generous gesture. Most won't expect anything, but you don't have to tip in money either. Sending a bottle of wine or a gift certificate for two to a nice dinner can be just as appreciated.

If a tip just doesn't fit into your budget, then find another way to show your gratitude: maybe it's an amazing and detailed Yelp review or referring a friend. Even handwritten thank-you notes let the people in your village know how much you appreciate all their hard work.

20 WEDDING ETIQUETTE RULES YOU CAN BREAK

Rules are meant to be broken, especially when said rules are old-fashioned and too numerous to count. Such is the case with wedding etiquette, so here are just a few of the rules you should totally take a pass on.

For starters, just because you're the bride doesn't mean your family should be expected to pay for everything. It's a super-old tradition. If your parents are able to pay, that's great, but they don't have to foot the whole bill. Both families can chip in, and even you and your beloved can add to the wedding fund.

Wearing white, having a veil, and donning sky-high heels are also rules you can firmly break. If you love white and have always dreamed of a veil, that's great, but it's also your wedding and you can choose whatever you want to wear for it.

Also, when putting together a registry, feel more than free to think outside the box—do you both want a gaming system? Add that on. Or would you rather have money for a honeymoon than a bunch of new plates? Go for it. It's up to you and yours what gifts you'd put to good use.

Some other rules you can totally break:

Don't feel obligated to have an equal number of attendants on each side—no one will notice or care.

Anyone can throw you a shower. So if your maid or man of honor is swamped, have another relative or friend throw one in your honor.

If you hate bouquet tosses, skip it.

Same with that whole garter thing.

When it comes to the rehearsal dinner, you can have one. Or you can do a brunch or lunch to cut costs. You don't need to feel obligated to invite all of your out-of-town guests—give them a list of restaurants in the area, and they'll be fine.

In terms of the honeymoon, you don't have to take it right away if it doesn't fit into your schedule. A "mini-moon" allows you to take a long weekend away and save the honeymoon for a later time.

Basically, whatever proper etiquette seems off to you, nix it. This is your day, and you get to make and break the rules for it.

culinary quests

ALL GREAT RELATIONSHIPS have the same things in common: dependability, trust, and a lot of love. And there's really no relationship more loving, dependable, and trustworthy than the one we have with food (and drink). Sweet, sweet coffee is there every morning to wake us up. And when we're tired at the end of a long day, all food wants is to wrap us in a giant spaghetti-noodle hug.

Isn't food the best? But what do we give food in return? Some of us eat a block of cheese for dinner instead of an actual meal. Others go to town on an endless breadstick basket at a chain restaurant instead of making bread from scratch. (So sorry, food! It's not you, it's convenience!) Yet the truth is that you can, in fact, use the fancy appliances in your kitchen.

So come on, get down on one knee and make the commitment. Whether it's cooking for one or hosting a girls' night in, master the basics so no one winds up with food poisoning. Or go even further and step up to the grill. You'll not only become invaluable at cookouts, you'll soon be grilling your own choice meats to perfection. After all, being food-and-drink savvy isn't all about impressing everyone else. It's about ensuring that absolutely nothing comes between you and the best food possible at the end of the day. Food and drink are in this relationship for the long haul, so it's time to give them the R-E-S-P-E-C-T they deserve.

1 KNOW THE ESSENTIAL PANTRY ITEMS

Much like the wardrobe that leads to Narnia, when you open your pantry door it can lead you to a new and exciting world of cooking. That's because pantry items are those basic supplies that almost all recipes call for. Meaning that when you want to cook, keeping these staples—think flour, tomato paste, and sea salt—around will ensure you're never far from a cooking adventure.

And getting to food adventure town just requires that you do some grocery shopping. Even if you may not want to buy things like canned tomatoes or jarred artichoke

THE PANTRY PARTY SHOULD INCLUDE

Vinegars, oils, and more

- Balsamic vinegar
- Beef broth stock
- Canola oil
- Chicken stock
- Honey
- Hot sauce
- Ketchup
- Maple syrup
- Mayonnaise
- Olive oil
- Soy sauce
- Vegetable stock
- Whole-grain mustard
- Worcestershire sauce

Canned and jarred

- Anchovies
- Canned artichoke hearts
- Canned cannellini beans
- Canned coconut milk
- Canned kidney beans
- Canned tomatoes
- Canned tuna
- Cocoa powder
- Jarred pesto
- Peanut butter

hearts because they don't seem "fresh," here's the thing: Those items are picked and canned at their peak, so you're not sacrificing quality by investing in them. They'll taste great, and you won't have to stress out about them going bad in your fridge. So whether you're whipping up a stir-fry or making a roast for a dinner party, make your life easier and keep around the pantry staples in the list below.

2   LEARN THE RATIOS FOR BAKING

Maybe you're already an excellent baker, or perhaps you're only excellent at eating baked goods. Either way, baking ratios are one of those lovely cooking tricks that will help you bake faster and eat those treats sooner.

A baking ratio is the basic measurement of which ingredients need to happen in order to get your baked goods going. Ratios are talked about in parts, like 3:2:1, 5:3, or 1:2:1. (Having any middle school math flashbacks?)

Grains

· Basmati rice	· Brown rice	· Oatmeal
· Breadcrumbs	· Couscous	· Saltines
	· Dried pasta	

Dry goods

· Almonds	· Cornstarch	· Potatoes
· Baking powder	· Dried yeast	· Sugar
	· Flour	

Spices

· Black pepper	· Dried oregano	· Ground cumin
· Chili powder	· Five-spice powder	· Sea salt
· Cinnamon	· Garlic powder	· Smoked paprika
· Curry powder	· Ground coriander	

EASY BAKING RATIOS

Biscuits	3:1:2	3 parts flour, 1 part fat, 2 parts liquid
Pie Dough	3:2:1	3 parts flour, 2 parts fat, 1 part water
Muffins	2:1:2:1	2 parts flour, 1 part fat, 2 parts liquid, 1 part egg
Pound Cake	1:1:1:1	1 part flour, 1 part fat, 1 part egg, 1 part sugar

If a ratio calls for three parts flour, two parts fat, it's talking about measurements. So, for example, if you were using three cups of flour, you'd use two cups of fat to keep that 3:2 ratio. And if a recipe called for two parts liquid, one part egg, the liquid you're using would need to be double the measurement of the whole egg. Make sense? Maybe? Read on.

What this all boils down to is that if you know the ratios for baking, you can whip things up easily without a recipe. And if you want to scale a recipe down, you can do that too. Let's use cookies as an example here, because they're so important in life. The ratio for cookies is 3:2:1, flour to sugar to fat. If you wanted to make a big batch, you would combine three cups of flour, two cups of sugar, and a cup of butter. But if you wanted to treat yourself to a "Cookies for Dinner Tuesday," you could still use that same 3:2:1 ratio and scale down to ¾ cup of flour, ½ cup sugar, and ¼ cup butter. And there you have it; some simple math can help you excel at baking and eating delicious cookies.

3 RECLAIM A CAST-IRON SKILLET

Cast-iron skillets are tough. Heck, they traveled on the Oregon Trail (the real one, not just the video game), and now they're practically living a life of leisure in your cabinet. But that doesn't mean they're indestructible. If, for

example, you're in a rush to get back to watching Netflix and accidentally leave that skillet to soak in water overnight, put it through the dishwasher, or try to wash it with soap, well . . . good luck not crying over the rust you'll see come morning.

While rust can be a little unsettling, it isn't the end of your cast iron. If your oven has a self-cleaning setting, simply put the skillet in the oven, and by the end of the cycle all of the rust will have turned to ash. Magic!

If you don't have that option, though, all you need is white vinegar, water, and a heavy-duty scrubbing brush (a copper pad, for example). Let the pan soak in a mixture of half vinegar, half water for up to six hours depending on the level of rust. Once it's done soaking, take your scrubbing brush and get to work. Either when the rust is all gone or your arms simply can't scrub any longer, you should stop.

No matter how you de-rust, make sure to reseason the pan once the rust is gone—coat it with lard, vegetable shortening, or bacon grease and then bake it in the oven at 220°F. A little tough love and your cast iron will be back to normal and ready to face the elements on the Oregon Trail once more. Let's just hope you don't lose any oxen.

4   CHOP AN ONION PROPERLY

There aren't many things that can make a grown woman cry, but there are onions, and no one is safe from those. You don't have to give an onion the satisfaction of your tears, though; just learn how to cut faster and properly so you can get what you need tear-free.

Before you get to chopping, there are a few prep steps to make your life easier. Put your onion in the freezer for fifteen to twenty minutes before you need it, and that will cut down on the buildup of sulfur gas (the stuff that makes you tear up). And use a large and sharp blade so you can easily cut without having to go back and cut again.

Now you're ready to chop. Start by cutting off the onion's stem, leaving the furry root end intact. Then cut the onion in half, not from the middle, but starting from the stem end. Once you have your half onion, peel away the outer layers. You should have half an onion with the root end in place, which means you're doing it right! Next cut lengthwise down the onion, stopping just before the root end, so the onion will remain in one piece.

If you want long onion slices, all you have to do is cut off the root end and you've got them. But if you're looking

to dice, make a few horizontal cuts through the onion and just before the root. Then cut vertically and parallel to the root across the onion until you have a mound of perfectly chopped onions that haven't been seasoned by your tears.

5   BREW A GREAT CUP OF COFFEE

Truth talk: The only reason we really bother waking up in the morning is for that first cup of hot coffee. And because coffee is such a vital part of each and every one of our lives, it's time to learn how to make the most of that first cup . . . then the second or third.

Start with the right tools, the most important of which will be your brewer. For ease and a sure-fire way to filter out oil and sediments that can often end up in your cup, use a manual dripper. This consists of a pot and a cone-shaped dripper. The process is simple: you put a filter in the cone dripper, fill it with coffee grounds (typically 1 tablespoon per 6 ounces of water), and pour boiling water over the grounds. You want to pour enough water to soak all of the coffee grounds, then let it filter through the cone and into the pot before adding more water.

If you need an alternative method, then invest in a French press—it's great at capturing a coffee's best flavors, and it also looks impressive on your kitchen countertop. Before you brew, you can boil water and pour it into the French press to warm it up, which can often be useful when you pour in the coffee grounds. After a few seconds, dump the hot water, and pour a few scoops of coffee grounds into the bottom of your press (a bit of experimentation will be required here, but aim for 1 to 2 tablespoons per every 6 ounces of water). When you're ready, take hot water and slowly pour it over the grounds. Let the grounds and hot water steep for four minutes if

it's a bigger brew, and two to three minutes for a smaller brew. There will likely be a layer of grounds that rises to the top. Feel free to scoop those out with a spoon so there's less of a chance they'll wind up in your cup. When it's done steeping, insert the press slowly and until it hits the bottom of the glass. Now you've got a cup (or two) of freshly pressed coffee waiting for you.

Aside from your brewer, you should also focus on the beans you're using. For the very best cup of coffee, buy coffee beans and grind them yourself just before you want to brew them. This will ensure not only a fresher-tasting coffee but also a more complex cup. If you don't like the taste of the tap water in your home, then take a cue from your taste buds and switch to filtered water when you're brewing. Keeping all that in mind should make your mornings a lot easier to wake up to.

6   SHAKE THE PERFECT COCKTAIL

A bartender, like any friend, knows how to get you a drink. But when it comes to a good cocktail, it's important to be your own best friend, and therefore your own bartender. The good news is that making a fancy shaken cocktail is a lot easier than it looks.

Let's start with your bartender tool belt. Find yourself a Boston shaker, which has a glass-and-metal shaker,

BASIC RATIOS FOR SHAKEN COCKTAILS

Margarita	1.5 ounces tequila, 1 ounce triple sec, 0.75 ounce lime juice
Whiskey sour	1.5 ounces whiskey, 1 ounce simple syrup, 0.75 ounce lemon juice
Sidecar	1.5 ounces brandy, 1 ounce triple sec, 0.75 ounce lemon juice
Mojito	2 ounces rum, 1 ounce lime juice, 1 ounce simple syrup (plus club soda to fill)

as opposed to the metal-on-metal Cobbler shaker (which can freeze together when using ice). Next comes a strainer so that you can avoid large ice chunks when you pour the drink. You'll also need a jigger for measuring your booze.

Speaking of booze, bars have all kinds of spirits to choose from, but for the purposes of your home bar, one of each of your faves will do the trick. A well-stocked bar (AKA your bar) will have a bottle each of gin, vodka, bourbon, brandy, rum, and Scotch.

Now that you've got the tools and ingredients, it's time to start mixing. To avoid diluting your cocktail too much, add all of the ingredients into the shaker first, saving the ice for last so it has less time to melt. Once the ingredients and ice are in, get your bartender face on and vigorously shake that tasty mix up for fifteen to twenty seconds. That's the perfect amount of time to dilute the drink, get it nice and cold, and make sure it's well aerated to provide the right cocktail texture.

Another easy trick is to match the temperature of the serving glass to the drink. So, for example, if you're making a hot toddy, pour hot water into the serving glass and dump it out before you add the drink in. If it's a cold beverage, store the glass in the freezer for a few minutes before serving.

When you've crafted your cocktail, it's time to take a sip and give the bartender a generous tip—after all, you've earned it.

7   MAKE A LEMON TWIST GARNISH

Is there anything quite as chic as an elegantly placed lemon twist on your drink? Twists are more than just a fancypants garnish, though—if prepared correctly, they also give your libation a nice aroma from the citrus oil, and even a touch of flavor.

Whether you're making a martini, whiskey sour, or sidecar, all you need is a lemon, bar spoon, and sharp knife to get started. Take your knife and cut the lemon in half horizontally, cutting through the middle rather than the ends. With half a lemon, cut a slice of lemon in the shape of a circle. The slice should be about as thick as the width of your pinkie nail. Now, using a bar spoon, cut out the fruit by wedging the spoon between the fruit and the edge of the rind. Do a full circle with the bar spoon, and the lemon fruit should be removed until you're left with the peel. Make a slice in the peel with your knife, and then twist the peel with your hands into a curlicue shape. It should be easy to twist, and if the lemon is fresh,

it will hold the shape. So all that's left to do is place the garnish on the rim and toast how chic you (and your drink) are.

8   FIND YOUR FAVORITE WHISKEY

Whiskey has traditionally been thought of as a man's drink, and it's time to change that. Not only is whiskey delicious, but the Scottish Gaelic word for whiskey, *uisge beatha,* literally translates to mean "water of life," and we could all use some of that.

Whiskey is a bit of an acquired taste because the flavors tend to be bold and rich, but the real key to being a whiskey drinker is finding the right bottle for you. Learning how to order a whiskey can really help that process.

For starters, decide if you want a cocktail, on the rocks, or neat. Go for the cocktail if you need something

EIGHT WHISKEYS YOU NEED TO TRY

- **Yamazaki Sherry Cask 2013:** rich and bold with a hint of spice
- **Glenfiddich Scotch 15 Year Old Solera Reserve:** hints of raisin, oak, and sherry
- **Four Roses Single Barrel:** flavorful with honey and brown sugar notes
- **Glenlivet 12 Year Old Single Malt Scotch:** creamy with apple and citrus flavors
- **Hudson Baby Bourbon Whiskey:** a smooth finish with corn and peppery elements
- **Noah's Mill Small Batch Kentucky Bourbon:** taste of almond and pine nut that goes well mixed in an Old Fashioned
- **Larceny Kentucky Straight Bourbon:** cinnamon and butterscotch notes
- **Pappy Van Winkle:** savor every drop you're lucky enough to find

to ease into that whiskey flavor. An old-fashioned is a great stirred cocktail, while a penicillin is shaken and can be made with Scotch, which is also super fun. And if Scotch versus bourbon is a little confusing, just know that they're both kinds of whiskey.

For the purposes of finding your favorite kind, though, order your whiskey neat—meaning served at room temperature and poured into a glass without ice or mixers. You can also opt for a whiskey on the rocks, which is whiskey poured over ice. And a lot of people think water brings out the flavor of whiskey, so ordering it with water is perfectly acceptable too.

In terms of taste, if you like things on the sweet side, ask for a spirit that uses corn. A lot of bourbons, like Four Roses, fall into this category. For a spicy taste, a rye whiskey, like WhistlePig or Wild Turkey Straight Rye Whiskey, will knock you off your feet in the best way possible. If you prefer a smoky flavor, then it's all about Scotch, whereas for a savory note, you'll want to try a Japanese whiskey.

If you're out and can't remember any of this, two basic things to look for are the color and smell. Generally, the darker the whiskey, the older it is, and how it smells is usually a solid indicator of what you're in for, taste-wise. No matter which one you order, you're drinking the water of life, so bottoms up.

9 STORE YOUR BOOZE

If stored properly, our booze will outlive us all. That's right, at the end of times it'll be zombies, a few human survivors, and all the hooch they can drink. Luckily, you don't need a cellar to store your wine and liquor—keeping a doomsday supply is much simpler than that.

We'll start with the hard stuff, the liquor and liqueurs. Unlike wine, you can store your spirits upright (there's no need to touch or preserve a cork) and at room temperature. Whether that storage space is on your bar cart or casually tucked in your desk at work is up to you. The only exception is vermouth, which is made with wine and needs to be refrigerated after opening. (Speaking of refrigeration, contrary to what your twenty-something friends may have told you, vodka does not need to be refrigerated at all.)

Another myth to dispel is that bottled liquors age over time. They don't, and in fact, the great thing about liquor is that once it's taken from the barrel and put in a glass bottle, it stops maturing. That means you can keep that unopened bottle around for as long as you like, and the taste won't change. If you do open your bottle, though, the contents will be exposed to the air and oxidize, so it's generally best to drink it within eight months to a year.

Wine, as many will know from personal experience, has a significantly shorter shelf life once opened: three days for sparkling, and five for reds and whites on average. That's because wine is a little more high-maintenance and takes just the right conditions to keep it at its best— not that high standards are a bad thing.

Storing wine with a natural cork has one big rule, and that's to keep the bottle on its side so the wine can touch that cork. A dry cork can let air in and change the taste of the wine, which you definitely don't want. A cool, dark place—think under 70°F, but above 45°F, and away from the sun's ultraviolet rays—is ideal for wine. The bottle shouldn't move around too much and, in general, some humidity is good (in the 50 to 80 percent range). The easiest solution is to buy a small wine cooler, but if you don't have that, the back of a closet or pantry will do the trick.

In an ideal world, wine would never go bad, and wine hangovers would be cured by eating hot fudge sundaes. But this is not that world, and the struggle of not being able to drink an entire bottle of wine in one night is real (for most of us, at least). Luckily, there are ways to save those precious drops for other important endeavors.

One option is wine ice cubes, which are exactly what they sound like and are made by pouring wine into an ice-cube tray. This is a great trick not only for enjoying wine on superhot days—sangria with sangria ice cubes, anyone?—but it's also wonderful for cooking. That way, whenever you have a recipe that calls for a quarter cup of wine, you'll have it at the ready without needing to open a new bottle.

Another option is to make a wine vinegar, which is terrific for cooking and salad dressings. Get a clean jar, add in mother of vinegar (which you can get from a raw apple cider vinegar, like Bragg's; it'll resemble a slimy floating blob), then your leftover wine, and about half the amount of vinegar to the wine you already added in. Cover the jar with a cheesecloth, seal it with a rubber band, and wait. Stir once a day, and start tasting it after a week—the vinegar should be good to go within two to four weeks.

So go ahead and open that new bottle . . . you'll find a way to finish it!

11 MAKE HARD CIDER

Know who's going to be impressed when you say that you brewed your own hard cider? Everyone. Making something from scratch is exciting, but it's even more exciting when it can get you buzzed.

There are two main components to hard cider, and unsurprisingly apple juice is one of them. You can buy a gallon of cider from the store—just make sure there's no sodium benzoate or potassium sorbate in the ingredients, as those preservatives kill yeast. You'll also need two gallon-size glass jugs to hold the cider (one jug if your cider comes in a glass jug), a funnel, a no-rinse sanitizer (like Star San), a stopper for the jar, an air lock, and yeast. You can buy all of this at your local homebrew store or online.

Follow your sanitizer's directions to clean the jar and funnel, then it's time to pour in your gallon of cider. Then add the yeast, which will eat up the sugars and produce all that alcohol and natural carbonation that makes hard cider so yummy over the course of a couple weeks. Whether you're using cider yeast or champagne yeast, just sprinkle about one-fifth of a five-gram yeast packet into your juice.

FERMENT

ONE MONTH

ENJOY!

So now we've got a sanitized, gallon jug filled with apple cider, and we've sprinkled yeast over the top of that juice. If you want to up the alcohol content, add in one-fourth cup of brown sugar—the more sugar, the higher the alcohol content. Just don't go overboard or add any spices until you taste the fermented cider.

Once you've settled on how hard the cider will be, it's time to move on to fermenting. Place the sanitized stopper into the jar and attach the air lock, which will let the CO_2 from the fermenting juice escape. Now place the jar out of direct light in a cool part of your house. A closet, or even a basement, works well.

Fermentation time varies but typically lasts a week to two weeks. After two days in the sealed jug, you'll see a whole lot of bubbling action happening in the cider, which is always a good sign. By day five, or sooner, your cider will be bubbling like crazy, and once that bubbling starts to die down, it means you're almost ready for the next step.

Once the bubbles in your cider have dwindled, it's time to move the cider into secondary fermentation and aging. If you want to purchase a siphon, that can make this step cleaner, but you can just carefully pour the cider from its jug to the second sanitized jug, leaving behind any sediment in the bottom. Once the cider is transferred, seal it in the second jar with a stopper and air lock and let it sit for about a month.

After roughly a month, your hard cider should be ready to drink. You can refrigerate it and serve it as is, which will be still (noncarbonated) hard cider. Or you can get more advanced and get into bottling if you'd like to create carbonated hard cider. Either way, it's sure to be a bragging right you can drink to.

It was the incomparable Betty White who said, "Vodka is kind of a hobby." And let's face it, she's right: vodka is delicious. Especially when served in a chilled martini glass and garnished with some choice olives.

But learning the delightfully easy art of infusing will take your vodka hobby to the next level. Infused vodka allows you to control what your alcohol tastes like.

Start by deciding what your vodka flavors will be. This will probably be the hardest part. Let's say you decide to make a strawberry-basil infused vodka, because that sounds delicious. Cut up enough strawberries to fill an airtight jar—look for a jar with a rubber seal—and layer basil leaves throughout. You don't need to fill every inch of the jar; after all, you'll need to allow some space for the vodka. Once the jar is filled, you'll pour in the vodka, leaving about a half inch of room between the ingredients and the lid. Close the lid of the jar and shake a few times to get it all mixed properly, then wait.

There's no exact science to when the infusion is finished; experimentation is key to finding what you like. However, the amount of time infusion takes really depends on the ingredients—strong ingredients, like tea, infuse quickly, while fruit can take up to a week. So give the jar a little shake every day, and even more important, give it a little taste starting after a few days. (It's a tough job, but someone has to do it!) When the

REALLY TASTY FLAVOR COMBOS TO TRY

- Bacon and habanero
- Basil and blueberry
- Cherry and cinnamon
- Cranberry and lime
- Earl Grey tea and cherries
- Figs and cinnamon
- Watermelon and mint

vodka is to your liking, all you have to do is strain out the ingredients, serve, and give a cheers to Betty White for being such a smart woman.

13 SCRAMBLE EGGS

Scrambled eggs are the Goldilocks of breakfast foods. They can't have a skillet that's too hot or too big, and they can't be seasoned too early. They need a skillet that's *just right* if you want perfectly fluffy eggs.

To please scrambled eggs' inner Goldilocks, there are a few tricks to know, starting with how you whisk. Whisk briskly until you see air bubbles form, which will help to get that fluffy consistency. Once in the pan, cook your eggs over low heat to avoid overcooking. Yes, it takes

longer—around ten minutes—but makes a huge differ-ence. And speaking of overcooked eggs, take them out of the skillet while they still look wet—not runny, but wet—as they continue cooking a bit when off the heat.

There are a few more Goldilocks tendencies to keep in mind with scrambled eggs. For example, wait to season with things like salt and pepper until the end of the cook-ing process, and use a pan that's the right size and not too large so your eggs won't spread too thin in the pan. To enhance the taste, there's often the tendency to add in things, like milk, but if you cook the eggs properly, you won't need it. And remember, when you cook scrambled eggs to perfection, you'll know, because they'll have that *just-right* taste.

14 CRAFT A CHEESE PLATE

Some of us live in the moment, while others live for the thought of a beautiful cheese plate in their future. We all have our thing!

Whether you're serving it up as a snack for guests or making a meal of it, a cheese plate is truly one of the best things in life. You don't need to go to a fancy cheese store to get your cheese plate right, either. (Though a trip to a fancy cheese store is always welcome!) You just need to know the basics of what to assemble to bring you into cheese-plate glory.

Really, you only need three types of cheeses to build a plate, especially if this is a solo trip to cheese-plate town. If you're hosting a larger gathering, up to five types of cheese work, but you certainly don't need more than that.

It's a great big cheese world out there, so you'll want to aim for a variety of textures and flavors with your cheeses. Include a soft cheese (like Brie or Camembert), a hard cheese (Jarlsberg or manchego), and an aged

cheese (aged cheddar or Comté) to help guide your decisions. Or you can make selections by buying cheeses made from different types of milk. So, for example, you could have a plate with cheeses made from goat, cow, and sheep's milk.

Then there's the noncheese stuff you can eat alongside the cheese to enhance the flavors. Include a variety of crackers or breads to add to the different textures you'll be experiencing, and an array of sweet and salty items, like walnuts, fig jam, honey, grapes, and salami, so you can mix and match flavors.

A few hand-selected cheeses, plus the fixings, and you've got yourself one world-class plate to look forward to (or enjoy right now).

The ability to make a homemade pasta sauce is one of the top three skills that will make you look like an impressive human being. Because when you can say you whipped up your own sauce, and it tastes like it was flown over from your great aunt's villa in Sicily, that's a real thing of beauty.

When creating a marinara sauce, you won't have to spend much time cooking, but you will have to wait while it simmers, bubbles, and cooks into something delightful. Before you get to that step, you'll need olive oil, an onion, seven garlic cloves, a few fresh basil leaves, sea salt, black pepper, and two 28-ounce cans of whole peeled tomatoes.

Once the ingredients are gathered, chop the onion and give the garlic a fine dice. Take out a large saucepan and pour in a tablespoon of olive oil to heat on medium. Add the onion and garlic and keep stirring them until the

onion turns translucent, and make sure not to let the garlic brown. Feel free to add another tablespoon of olive oil if you need to. Once the garlic and onion are cooked, add in both cans of tomatoes, a pinch of black pepper and sea salt, and top with a few basil leaves.

For the next 45 minutes, you're going to keep the pot on low heat, letting the sauce simmer and occasionally stirring. Make sure the tomatoes are getting crushed and stewed into the sauce, and sneak tastes to make sure it doesn't need any extra salt or pepper. When the time is up, remove the pan from heat, and coat some really yummy pasta with the sauce. You can top each plate with an extra basil leaf if you want to get super fancy, but otherwise just enjoy the fact that you're a person who doesn't need jarred sauce.

Have extra? Marinara freezes well, so you can cover up and store whatever you don't use and reheat it for the next time you need a pasta dinner. Or, you know, you can eat the leftovers the same week!

16 COOK A TURKEY

To cook a turkey is truly a labor of love, as you've likely seen on any given holiday and many a TV show and movie. If you've decided to take on the task this year, a good place to start is to make sure the turkey is properly defrosted. It takes twenty-four hours to thaw every four pounds in the fridge, so plan ahead to make sure you're set the day of. Once defrosted, remove the giblets, then rinse the turkey with cold water and pat dry with paper towels. If you don't plan to cook the bird immediately, store it in the fridge in a container that prevents the juices from dripping on any other food.

Now bring on the butter. You'll want to melt a stick of butter and season with two teaspoons each of any

fresh herbs you may want (rosemary and sage are great options). You may not use all of the herbed butter, depending on turkey size, but gently lift the skin above the breast meat and load the area between the meat and skin with the herbs and butter. Use any remaining butter to coat the top of the turkey, and season with salt and pepper.

To make sure the turkey is evenly cooked, tuck the wingtips underneath the turkey, and truss the turkey by tying the legs together with twine. For an extra moist and mouthwatering turkey, soak a cheesecloth in butter and place it over the top of the turkey.

Heat the oven to 325°F and place your bird in a roasting pan on the lowest rack, and check every hour (without opening the oven!) to make sure nothing's on fire. Remove the cheesecloth once it turns brown, and wait for the thermometer in the breast meat to hit 165°F. Once it does, you'll remove the turkey and be greeted by a flourish of applause from your guests, because that, my friend, is the work of a Turkey Queen.

17 USE A CHARCOAL GRILL

Much like state parks and Ryan Gosling, grilled burgers are our greatest natural resource, and it's our duty to help that natural resource flourish. As you can see, learning to operate a charcoal grill is imperative.

Step one is lighting the grill, which is arguably one of the hardest parts and also why you should invest in

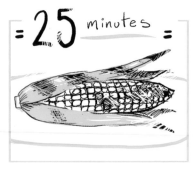

a chimney starter. Chimney starters are easy and quick to use. All you need to do is load the charcoal into the chimney starter, add newspaper, and light as directed. Once you see flames, pour the charcoals onto the grill and wait for them to burn grey. That ashy color is exactly how you want your coals to look before you begin cooking. Oh, and ensure that they're distributed evenly along the bottom grate.

Manning—or better yet, womanning—the grill is mostly about controlling the temperature of those coals. The way you do that is through the vents on the grill—the more oxygen the coals get, the hotter they'll burn. So if you need more heat, open the vents, and if you're looking to cool it down, partially close those vents. Close the vents completely only when you're ready to extinguish the coals.

Once the coals reach your desired temperature, start grilling! Keep in mind that seafood and beef tend to cook at a higher temperature for a shorter amount of time, while pork and chicken cook at medium heat for a longer amount of time. You'll get the hang of it, and you'll become a grilling ambassador in the process.

18   MAKE WHIPPED CREAM

Do you believe in magic? How about the magic that happens when you take two ingredients, put them in a bowl, and a few minutes later have fluffy, delicious whipped cream?

It's true! Making whipped cream requires only two ingredients: sugar and heavy whipping cream. The real secret, though, is to make sure your ingredients are as cold as possible so the cream doesn't melt. That means you shouldn't let your heavy whipping cream sit out at room temperature for too long, and you should put the

mixing bowl and whisk into the freezer for ten minutes before starting. If you have an electric mixer, then you can detach the beaters and put those into the freezer as well.

As soon as everything is very cold, pour a cup of heavy cream into the mixing bowl and whisk vigorously (or by machine) for a few minutes until the cream doubles in thickness. Once that's accomplished, add in two table-spoons of sugar and beat until it reaches peak whipped cream consistency. Grab a wand—er, spoon—dig in, and know that you've just made a little magic in a bowl.

19   SET A TABLE

If you've ever seen Julia Roberts in *Pretty Woman*, then you know there's plenty to learn when it comes to a table setting. Luckily, there are some basic how-to rules you can follow. (That way, the next time you're out to dinner with a billionaire, you'll know which fork is for the salad.)

The easiest part comes first: The plate will always be the center of your setting and placed in the middle no matter what. For a basic table setting, you'll put the fork to the left of your plate, then your knife to the right with the blade side facing toward the plate. Above the knife, you can put your water glass or wineglass. Place a spoon next to the knife, and the napkin should be folded on top of the plate or put to the side of the fork.

For a setting that's on the fancier side, the general idea is to build a setting where you can work from the

outside in with the utensils and plates. So start again with your main plate in the middle. (At least this one thing is easy to remember!) If you have multiple courses, stack the plates in order, from first-course plate (salad or appetizer) on the top, going all the way down to the largest or main-course plate. If you want to include a plate for rolls, place that plate in the left corner of the setting with a butter knife on top of the plate. Forks will again go on the left side of the plate, with the first fork to be used (salad fork) on the outside, and the dinner fork on the inside, closest to the plates. While the knife will still be placed to the right of the plate and facing in, any spoons you'll be using will be placed next to it, to the right. If you plan on having dessert, then put the utensils for that horizontally just above the plates. Place your water glasses and wineglasses above the knife and spoons and to the right of the dessert utensils, with the finishing touch being the napkin on top of the plates or underneath the forks.

20   HOST A DINNER PARTY

In the Venn diagram of your friends and nice things, there is the dinner party smack in the middle. The only problem with a dinner party is that instead of cooking for yourself, you're going to be cooking for a larger group. Oh, you'll also have to entertain and make your house look like something other than the place where you like to take your bra off.

So, how can you host a dinner party and not lose your will to live? Keep the guest list small, and select people to come who you know will get along. You don't want to spend all this time cooking and preparing only to realize five minutes in that your friend who likes to talk about sexual conquests is sitting next to the one person who finds that repulsive. Just think ahead, and cap the head count at eight people.

This may go without saying, but be considerate of your guests. So ask about any food allergies or dietary restrictions before you plan the menu, and do assigned seating with cutesy place cards. While the food is obviously a highlight of the meal, it's the company and making sure the conversations are flowing that will really make the night memorable.

Some small details that can add a lot of ambiance to the party are a great music playlist to have in the background and small decorations to line your table—that can be anything from candles to your vintage salt and pepper shakers.

When guests arrive, the stress of making sure they feel taken care of will come out to play. If you plan to have a cheese plate or some kind of appetizer before the meal, serve it in a space that isn't the dinner table. Have people stand and mingle, or sit in the living room while nibbling so you can have time to prep the main dish. Prep as much as you can ahead of time so you have less work the night of. That can mean setting the table the night before, or assembling the meal in advance so the only work you have involves putting it in the oven. To take more off your plate, so to speak, feel free to also ask some of your more trusted guests to bring wine or dessert so the burden of the party isn't solely on you.

In the end, this is a night that involves you, your friends, and food, so nothing can really ruin that.

get
creative

AH, PINTEREST, the place where being creative looks as easy as wishing it were so. But any discerning woman knows that adding lace to a dress doesn't simply happen by whistling a merry tune while woodland creatures come to sew it for you. Nor does a handmade blanket appear out of thin air every time you sit in a rocking chair. To be a crafter, you can't rely on magic; you must dive knitting-needle- or pen-and-ink-first into the creative side of your brain.

Tapping into your artistic side often means letting go of the idea that crafting is only for certain types of people. Or that it's too hard to get into. As an intelligent woman with varied interests, there will be times in your life when knowing how to make something will be an asset. Maybe it will be stenciling your own wall art instead of paying a small fortune for someone else to do it. Or maybe it will be as simple as adding a welcoming "Uteruses before Duderuses" cross-stitch to your home décor.

No matter, the truth is that crafting isn't old-fashioned or stuffy, it's whatever you make of it (literally). So if you want to convert the branch of a fallen oak tree into some badass coasters, boom: that's how you craft. If you'd rather modernize some boring gloves by turning them into fingerless ones, then get after it. And you don't need anyone else to blend your chalkboard paint, because with a little practice, you'll be doing that all on your own. Crafting doesn't have to take hours, and it doesn't have to be something that's only a dream as you click through photos online.

1 PAINT YOUR FABRIC COUCH

"As you wish" doesn't have to be just a line from a movie. When you learn how to paint your couch—yes, paint a couch, which doesn't sound right, but it totally is—then your couch will be saying, "As you wish!" every time you feel like a change. If you want to get a totally fresh look for much less cash than buying a new piece of furniture, then read on.

While you can also paint leather couches—doubly crazy, right?—this tutorial is specifically for how to paint an upholstered fabric couch. Start by mixing your couch paint, which will be a can of whatever paint color you love, blended with fabric textile medium, which you can buy at most craft stores. For every quart of paint, you'll need 16 ounces of fabric textile medium. So if it's a particularly large couch, you may need 2 quarts of paint and 32 ounces of medium.

After the paint and medium are mixed, and before you pour it straight out of the can, dampen the couch fabric to ensure that the paint won't run. Fill a spray bottle with water and spritz away at the section of couch you plan to paint first. Once that section is damp, wait a minute for it to penetrate.

A regular paintbrush or foam brush will do the trick when applying the paint. Just move section by section, spritzing with water and then painting, so you're working on a damp canvas. Apply the first coat, and give it a full day to dry before applying a second. Oh, and it's a good idea to test the paint on a lesser-seen section, should something in the application not go according to plan.

Once the paint is dry, take a piece of fine-grit sand-paper and rub it over the fabric to soften it up, as you've sort of created a painted canvas to sit on, which can often feel a bit stiff at first. Sanding the couch will create dust, so wear a dust mask and wipe any dust off with a towel. You can also do this in between coats to soften as you go. Either way, you'll be making your boring old couch into a work of art.

1

2

3

4

2 **RE-COVER A THROW PILLOW**

Some of us are traditional and eat at the table, while others need to keep watching Netflix and thus sit on the couch and use a decorative throw pillow as a makeshift table. If you're in the latter group, you'll occasionally need to redo those pillows, if only so you don't feel bad every time you spill something.

Making a new pillow cover doesn't need to be a needle-and-thread endeavor. There's a no-sew technique that will give you a totally new pillow to hold and place your snacks on before you know it. First pick whatever fabric you want to cover your pillow with—something solid,

5

6

7

8

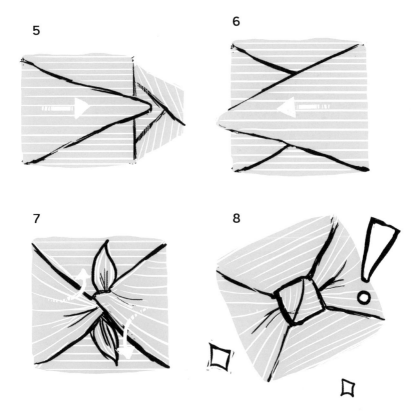

something gingham, really whatever you want. Just make sure the fabric is three times as wide as your pillow and twice as long. Once you have that, lay the fabric on a flat surface with the side you want to show to the world facing down. Place your throw pillow on top of the center of that fabric. Then fold the bottom and top halves of the fabric over the pillow—they should hit just about the center of the pillow.

At this point, the pillow should be fully covered by fabric, and there should be excess fabric on the right and left sides of the pillow. On one side, take the outside corners of the excess fabric, and fold them towards each other so they form a triangle. You'll repeat that action on the opposite side.

Once you have your triangles, bring one across, then the other, so they're both resting on top of the pillow. To finish this project off, all you have to do is tie the triangles in a square knot by taking the fabric over-under, then under and over.

See, no needle or thread required for a one-of-a-kind decorative pillow–snack table.

3   STENCIL WALL ART

If you want fancy art on your wall but don't personally know how to make said art, look no further. With the help of a beautiful stencil, it will seem as if you hired a master painter to transform your space. (Only you and your stencil will know the truth!)

Picking a stencil is obviously the first step, so visit your local craft stores to kick this project off. There are all kinds of patterns, including chevron, florals, and various geometric shapes—just find the one that speaks to you. While shopping, you'll also want to buy the appropriate paint. Most latex and acrylic paints will do the job, as will stencil creme and spray paint (though spray paint can be a little unruly if you've never used it before). The only kind to really avoid is oil paint, which can take a long time to dry and can drip slightly.

As with any painting job, you'll want to clear the room of objects you love so they don't accidentally get doused, and rub the walls down with a towel to remove any dust or fibers that can get in the way of you and your beautiful stencils.

Once the walls are cleared, secure the stencil to the wall at the top and center of the space you're working on

using an adhesive spray or painter's tape. A quick measure of the room with measuring tape should help you find that center top spot if you're having trouble. When the stencil is secured, make note of the registration marks that are likely at the corners of your stencil. Mark those with a pencil so that as you move, you know where the edges should fall.

Now it's time to paint! When picking a brush to create your masterpiece, consider the size of the stencil and the design—does it have intricate details that might need a smaller brush?—that will help you choose the right tool for your canvas. As you paint, remember that less paint is more to ensure your stencils bleed less. Once you've finished a row, remove the stencil and move across with the knowledge that soon you'll be a woman with fancy art from a master painter (wink) on her walls.

4 CREATE A CHALKBOARD WALL

If you think chalkboard paint is not for you, consider the fact that chalkboard paint no longer has to be black. Now, with homemade paint, you can create whatever color canvas you want on whatever color wall you like.

Chalkboard paint can be a little pricey in the store, but it just has two ingredients: paint and nonsanded tile grout. To make your own batch, pick a paint color (black, blue, magenta), and combine it with the tile grout. The basic recipe for that is with every cup of paint, mix in 2 tablespoons of tile grout. So for a quart of paint, you'd need 8 tablespoons of grout, and so on.

Once the homemade chalkboard paint is mixed well, go ahead and paint the surface you plan to use with it. You may need two to three coats of the stuff, since chalkboard paint can be on the thinner side. When the surface is good and coated, let it cure for a solid two days.

Next comes the part that will bring you back to childhood, because you're going to cover the entire wall with chalk, then erase it. This will help seal the paint and make sure you have many writable nights ahead of you. To do this, use the side of a piece of chalk to rub it across the chalkboard paint and cover it completely. When the wall is covered, and that piece of chalk is whittled down to a nub, take a cloth, Magic Eraser, or chalkboard eraser, and clean off all of your chalk art.

Don't worry. You'll be able to draw and write all of the important stuff down again immediately after you erase that first coat of chalk. Doodle away!

5 CRAFT YOUR OWN STREAMER GARLAND

Want to throw a fancy shindig without breaking the piggy bank wide open? Try upgrading your party with an easy DIY streamer garland.

If you ever made paper snowflakes in grade school, then you know the incomparable art of cutting shapes out of paper. Which is the exact beauty of this craft— all you'll need are streamers and scissors. Much like the snowflake trick, you're going to roll out your streamer and then fold it into napkin-size squares, layering each square on top of the other so it looks like one neat pile of paper squares, or an accordion. Keep folding until you have a medium-size stack.

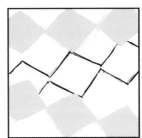

Next, and arguably the most fun part, is deciding on the shape you're going to cut out—scallops, small triangles, a diamond, or whatever you think up! Pick a shape and draw the outline on the top of the pile to guide your cutting, and when you're ready, carefully cut along the shape. The goal is to have a string of shapes still intact and not individually cut, so don't forget to leave room for the actual garland part. To do that, you want to ensure the folds remain intact—in other words, don't cut into the fold line that keeps the paper string connected. When you unfold the stack, you should have a beautifully fashioned garland to string across the walls—perfect for a party, fancy or otherwise.

6 MAKE WOOD SLICE COASTERS

Of course we put ourselves on pedestals, but what about our drinks? They deserve to be worshipped as well. Hence the beauty of a DIY coaster: It's a pedestal you've made to treat that drink like the queen it is.

The main ingredient needed for this DIY is in your own backyard. To make the beautiful wooden coasters of your dreams, you'll of course need wood. There's no particular type that's ideal, but if it has a nice grain (the pattern of the wood), that's something to look out for. Pine, oak, olive, aspen, and cedar are all solid (get it?) options. You'll want to nab thicker branches to get the right length and diameter, so you have something that can support your drinking glass.

Next you'll cut that branch into manageable pieces with a handsaw or an electric saw. A half-inch depth, give or take, is ideal to steady your drinks on. Use sandpaper on each side of the cut wood to smooth it out so your glasses don't need to hold on for dear life. And to finish, coat the coaster with a Danish oil or other wood oil of your choosing to protect it from moisture getting in. Now place that fancy drink on top and admire your work!

7 THE DIY WINE RACK

There's so much wine in the world and so little time to drink it. While you're stockpiling all those beautiful bottles for later consumption, you'll surely need your own personal cellar for storing them.

Start your cellar off by heading to a craft store to buy a wooden crate—the bigger the crate, the more bottles it will hold. If the color of the crate isn't perfect, a wood stain can change it so that it makes sense in your space. Once you've stained the wood, the real DIY of this project begins. Since it's not ideal to just stack wine bottles on top of each other, as you don't want your bottles to crack, create separate spaces within the crate to allow some breathing room. Do this by purchasing a piece of wood board—which should be wide enough to reach the front and back of the crate—and create an *X* shape inside the box.

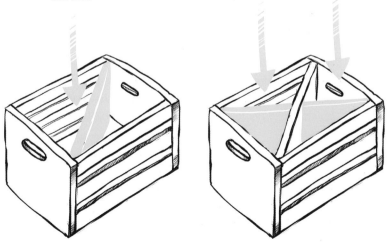

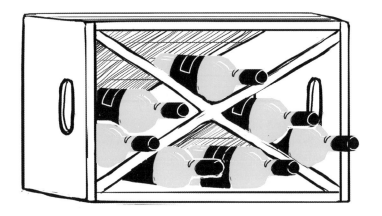

To get that *X*—which divides the crate into four sections—start by making the first diagonal line of the *X*. You'll do this by measuring and fitting part of the board to form a diagonal line from one corner of the crate to another. Now you have one line of the *X*. Two shorter pieces of board will meet in the middle to form the second diagonal line—the result being three pieces of wood that form an *X* shape.

Once you've measured out your *X* shape, you can stain those diagonal pieces as well if you want them to match. When they're ready to be firmly placed, you can secure them to the crate with nails, wood glue, and wood filler. When those have all dried, take a piece of sandpaper and sand around the crate to make sure everything is smooth for your valuable bottles. After all, you want to make sure your cellar is prepped for whatever refined bottles you bring to it.

8 ADD LACE TO YOUR CLOTHES

Lace deserves a raise. It's the hardest-working fabric there is, because while it can be incredibly sexy, it's also

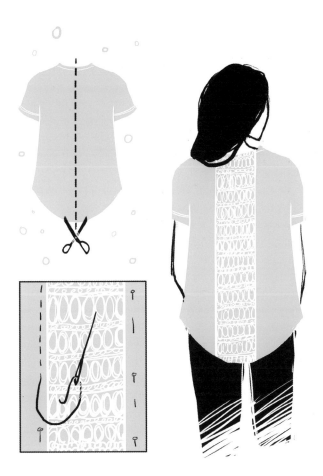

an easy way to dress up clothing and add room to items that no longer fit. (We're rooting for you, lace!)

To add some lacy appeal to a shirt, jeans, or whatever else needs revamping in your wardrobe, start by gathering up the basics: lace fabric, scissors, sewing pins, and a needle and thread. Then measure the area you want to cover in lace—maybe it's the sleeves, the collar of a shirt, or a whole panel. Once you've measured and cut the appropriate size for the lace, pin the lace edges to your clothing. Or, if you are revamping shorts by adding a lace trim to each leg, you'd pin the top of the lace inside the short legs where you plan to sew it. Then all you need to do is string a needle and thread, and start stitching. Begin at the end of one part of your fabric and use enough stitches so that the lace is securely held in place. When you reach the other end, cut off any excess lace you may have, tie off the thread, and give a round of applause for lace.

If you want to add a few more inches of give to a piece of clothing by using lace, the process is very similar. Say you want to resize a shirt; you'd start by taking scissors and going straight up the back to create a back lace panel. Only go up as far as you want the lace panel to go, and the higher you cut, the more room you'll make. One you've made the cut, measure and pin the lace to the inside of the shirt. Keep the pins in place and remove them as you sew until your new lace panel is carefully sewn into the shirt. Keep in mind that adding the lace will change the shape and flow of the shirt, so if it feels too snug or too loose, you can always remove the panel and start again. You've now saved yourself the hassle of buying a new shirt and added your own unique design in the process.

9   MAKE A NO-SEW FLEECE BLANKET

Ah, a warm blanket. The mere sight of one is enough to make you want to curl up and live happily underneath it forever. Since it'll be your forever home, why not make one to your exact specifications?

All you need are scissors and fleece fabric, which you can get at your local craft store. Pick a pattern and ask the store staff to cut two pieces of fabric that are both two yards long.

With the supplies secured, start by laying the two pieces of fabric one on top of the other on a flat surface, with the sides you want to face out doing exactly that. And

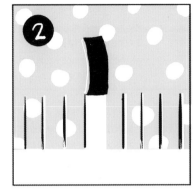

as there may be some jagged or patchy edges, use scissors
to cut along the sides of the fabric to even them out.

Once they're even, cut a square about two inches deep
from all four corners of the fabric. Then you'll go along
each side and make slits that will look like fringe. These
slits should be an inch wide and two inches long. As you
cut, fold each strip over the fabric and make sure that
you're cutting both pieces of fabric so that each slit lines
up perfectly with the next.

With the folded strips, cut a small slit in the center
of every fold. Once you have the center slits, you're going
to take a folded strip and pull the top of it through the

center slit of the fabric. As you pull the fabric through the slit it will form a knot—make sure to pull it tightly through so the knot stays intact. Continue down each side until all of the strips are knotted, and you'll have yourself a cushy new friend to cuddle up to.

10   NAIL THE PERFECT CROSS-STITCH

A "Be Nice or Leave" cross-stitch would make a perfect addition to any home. But in order to become a cross-stitch master and craft the perfect message for your dwelling, you have to learn the basics first.

For cross-stitch beginners, you'll need a fourteen-count piece of Aida cloth (cross-stitch fabric), a needle, scissors, and whatever color of cotton craft floss you like. Begin by cutting a twelve-inch piece of floss and removing two strands from the six-strand floss. Those two together are what you'll be stitching with. Grab your needle and thread the strands through that needle, forming a loop and knotting the ends of the loop together.

Bring your needle and floss up through the back side of the Aida cloth, pulling up to remove any slack, but not bringing the knotted end all the way through the fabric. In other words, you want it to stay in place. To complete your stitch, bring the needle into the hole diagonally down

IDEAS FOR WHAT TO CROSS-STITCH

- "Pasta Bowls Not Gender Roles"
- "Blessed to Have Breasts"
- "You Know Nothing, Patriarchy"
- "Well-Mannered AF"
- "Ramen > Men"

and to the right of where your needle first came up. Once you've found your spot, bring the needle through to the back side and pull away any slack.

You should now have one diagonal stitch. To finish the cross-stitch, insert the needle immediately above the stitch you just made through the back side. Then insert the needle diagonally down and to the left of the hole you came up through. There should now be one perfectly completed *X* on the front of your Aida cloth. Now you have your first official cross-stitch, the first step toward cheeky cross-stitch fun.

11 MAKE A YARN-STRIPED VASE

When the crafting history books are written, yarn vases will go down as one of the easiest DIY projects. Whether you want to decorate for football season in your team's

colors, or wear your Hogwarts house pride on your vase, this craft allows you to customize in so many ways.

For this one, you'll need a vase or jar, yarn in whatever color you like, double-sided tape, scissors, and tacky glue. Start by wrapping the vase or jar in the double-sided tape, leaving half-inch gaps between the rows of tape. If you want any part of your vase to be clear of yarn, then leave that tapeless.

With your tape in place, it's time to get colorful. Grab the yarn and start by wrapping the color you want at the bottom of the jar. Make sure to press down on the yarn where it hits the tape to firmly secure it, and feel free be meticulous or wild with the look of the yarn here. To switch colors, simply snip your yarn with the scissors, and bust out your new yarn color. If you need to secure any loose yarn—like the beginning and ends—use a dollop of the tacky glue.

Before you know it, your Hufflepuff vase is complete and ready to be proudly displayed to all who enter.

12 CREATE A TERRARIUM

Have you ever wanted to be the master of your own universe but aren't *totally* sure where to begin? Enter the terrarium, where you control what goes in and are queen of the terrarium realm

A terrarium is a bit like a fishbowl, in that you can craft the surroundings and put it on your desk to keep you company. To get started, you'll need a glass container, which can be anything from a mason jar to an actual terrarium pot. Once you have a container, the basic elements of a terrarium are pebbles, charcoal, and soil. So create a base using a layer of pebbles, then a layer of charcoal that's about a fourth as deep as that of the pebbles, followed by a layer of soil that's half the depth of the pebbles.

Now you have your base, and the terrarium is entirely open for your creative interpretation. You can add in plants, like succulents, a cactus, bromeliad, moss, or ferns, and leave it at that—a lovely, plant-filled terrarium. Or if you want to step up your game, you can create a little world, adding a plastic animal or three of your choosing. Maybe even throw in some other cute décor and a DIY banner. If you have a sealable container, water the terrarium, close the lid, and you never need to worry about it again. But if the terrarium is in an open container, be mindful to water it every few days.

13 TREAT YOURSELF TO AN EYE PILLOW

You're a queen, which means you woke up like this. But for those days when you know waking up is going to be a little rougher than usual, treat yourself to a soothing eye pillow.

Depending on what level of luxury you plan to treat yourself to, you can use cotton or silk for your eye pillow. Either one will allow breathability; you just need a 16x4-inch rectangle of your chosen material. Once you've secured that, fold the material in half, so it's still a rectangle, and sew around the edges, leaving a half-inch opening on one end. Use that opening to tuck the material through, turning the eye mask inside out so the stitching is on the inside and not touching your face.

Through that same hole, stuff the pillow with any manner of things to help you unwind. You can either use rice or flaxseed to fill the pillow, about one and a half cups or until it feels full enough to do the job. Place the rice in a bowl and add in fifteen drops of essential oils, like lavender or dried chamomile, before filling the pillow. When you're done, sew up the hole, pop it in the microwave for fifteen seconds, lie back, and treat yourself to that mask. Your body will thank you for it.

14 DESIGN A CUT-OUT T-SHIRT

There are few things more classic than a classic tee. It's versatile, can be dressed up or down, and unless you've been living under a rock in an alternate universe, you likely own one. While there's nothing wrong with maintaining

the integrity of a classic, there's also something very fun about the idea of spicing one up with a cut-out design.

All you'll need is a tee, construction paper, and scissors to get the job done. To start, decide what you want your cutouts to be—hearts, diamonds, maybe a sleek triangle—and create those shapes on the construction paper. Cut the shapes out, fold your tee inside out, and place the shapes wherever you want them to be on your shirt. A series of triangle cutouts around the neckline looks incredible, as does a trio of cut-outs down the back of a shirt, for example. Next you're going to trace the outline of the shapes with an erasable marker so it doesn't permanently stain your top.

Once your design is traced, go ahead and cut along the outlines until you've got your newly styled top. Classic never looked this bold.

15   CUT FINGERLESS GLOVES

Let's start a petition here and now to ban the cruel and unusual punishment that our fingers have to endure every winter. I'm talking, of course, about being trapped by the confines of gloves. Go ahead, sign the petition and set those fingers free with some fingerless gloves.

To get the best fit possible, start by putting a glove on your hand. That way you can identify the cut points—do you want the glove to end just after your first knuckle, the second, or maybe have it stop at the top of your palm? Wherever you decide to cut, remember that the fabric will roll back slightly from that point. So cut higher than you think you should, because you can always cut more off if you need to.

Next, make your cut marks. Take your fabric scissors and cut along the point where you want your fingers to pop out on each finger of the glove. You don't have to cut all the way through, but make a mark so that when you take the glove off, you know where to go. Then remove the glove and snip off whatever amounts you have left. Now you've got a glove without the fingers, and at this point, you can use your one cut glove as a blueprint for the other glove, and cut accordingly.

It's up to you to decide if you want the ends to be rolled down or slightly frayed. If slightly frayed, chop off the rolled part until it lays flat on your fingers. If rolled, you can leave as is, or take an extra step and stitch the rolled ends into the glove so they stay in place. When you're done, your fingers will be free from the confines of winter wear.

16 GLITTER YOUR SHOES

How many times have you clicked your heels together, said, "There's no place like home," and still *not* immediately been transported to Kansas? A lot, probably. While teleportation isn't a reality (yet), snagging those iconic glittery heels is within reach.

To start, pick the shoe you want to gussy up, and use a paper towel to wipe off any hidden dirt or fibers. Cover the surface you'll be working on in newspaper to make for easy glitter cleanup, and stuff the insides of the shoes with tissue so the glitter doesn't get in. Once you've done that, apply fabric or jewel glue to the shoe in sections with a foam brush. You want to go section-by-section so the glue doesn't dry before you can glitter it up.

When you've got one section covered in glue, bring out the glitter! You can stick to one color or mix for a rad combo. Either way, you'll be sprinkling the glitter over one glue-covered section at a time. As that dries, apply the next coat of glue to a new section, and repeat the process of glue then glitter until your shoe is covered.

If the first coat isn't enough glitter for your liking, wait a few hours for the shoe to dry. Once it has, you can apply a second coat of glue, then glitter, to get it as sparkly as you like.

When you're done, click your heels together and know there's no place like a glittered shoe place.

17 CREATE A CUSTOM PHONE CASE

For better or worse, your phone is always by your side. It stores your photos, sends emails, and blares extra loud—sometimes multiple times—each morning to make sure you don't oversleep. Since you spend so much time staring at your phone, you should make it look exactly how you want it to.

The trick to a custom case is that you want it to feel uniquely you, without having to painstakingly craft for hours to get it. Enter washi tape, a great material to DIY

with because it's both paper and masking tape, which means you get to choose the patterns, colors, and position. Plus, it's just as easy to remove as it is to apply, so you can switch up the colors whenever the mood strikes.

Head to a craft store to pick the washi tape of your dreams, and for the purposes of this DIY, you'll pick three different colors. With these three complementary colors, you can make any number of patterns on your phone case. Alternate vertical or horizontal lines with your tape, create a series of diagonals, or cut rows of tiny washi squares to form a grid. Whatever pattern you decide on, use scissors to cut the tape when you're ready to apply it.

Remember, washi tape is easy to remove, so if you decide to change the pattern, it will be an easy fix. And hey, you can always set a monthly reminder on your phone to change out the colors (if you want).

18 WRAP A GIFT LIKE A PRO

Do you have gift-wrapping anxiety? You know, because every time you try to wrap a gift, one side bubbles out. Or there's too much paper. And you don't know why, but you've somehow run out of paper, even though you measured it.

Sweat the wrapping no more, because there's a foolproof way to make it look like you're a wrapping prodigy!

Start by placing your gift on a sheet of wrapping paper and making sure there's enough on all four sides to cover the gift plus an extra inch more. Cut off that size, and place your gift at a diagonal on the paper. Now two edges of the gift should be touching two sides of the paper, and there should be a triangle formed with the paper on the outside of the gift. Fold the two corners nearest to your gift over—they should look like two triangles—and secure them to your gift with tape.

GET CREATIVE

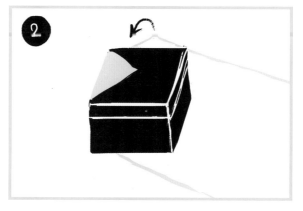

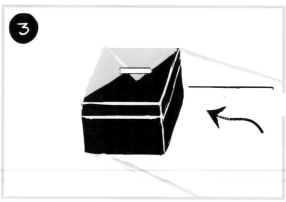

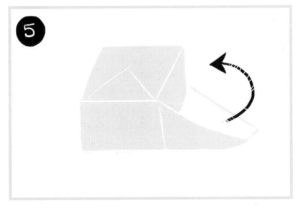

Now fold the largest piece of wrapping paper up and over the gift, and flip your gift over. You should now see another two triangles formed, and you'll fold one, then the other, and secure them both with tape to the gift.

Before you know it, a perfectly wrapped gift will be looking back at you, all without so much as a paper cut.

19   SELECT FLOWERS FOR A BOUQUET

Roses are red, violets are blue, make your own homemade bouquet, and you'll brighten someone's day. OK, that wasn't the best poem, but knowing how to craft a bouquet does guarantee you'll be able to control the look and message of a bunch of flowers (no poetic skills required).

Before you start the bouquet, think about the message you want to send with your arrangement. If it's a thank-you bouquet, then whites, purples, and greens can convey your intent—flowers like heather, sweet pea, lisianthus, and aster are a good combination. Whereas if you're trying to tell someone you are smitten, aim for red flowers—the color of passion—with options like red tulips, celosia, dahlia, and chrysanthemums. Whatever the message, take a few moments to research flower meanings and color combinations so your bouquet packs an extra special something.

Once you decide on the meaning and types of flowers to include, you'll need eighteen to twenty stems of a hardy flower, a sharp knife to even out the ends, a rubber band or ribbon to tie it all together, and a piece of parchment paper to prevent any drips.

Use a knife or cutter to trim off any excess thorns or leaves left on each stem. Then pick four flowers to be the center of the bouquet and arrange them in a square at even heights. Build out the bouquet around those center four, going flower by flower, until you've used all of the stems and created a full, round bouquet. At this point, you can trim the bottoms of the stems so the length is even and manageable. Then secure the arrangement with a rubber band or bow, and wrap it up in parchment paper. It's impossible to know what will be more satisfying— that you built something so beautiful or that you're about to make someone's day.

body talk

YOU SHOULD ABSOLUTELY treat your body as a temple. Worship it, create a shrine to it, and shower it with the finest things in life. After all, we only get the one, right?

That doesn't mean we all want the same thing, though—and it's fine that we all have different definitions of what our own temple should look like. Maybe for your perfect self, you want to wear heels but you don't want the blisters. Or perhaps your temple requires a natural DIY deodorant without those added chemicals that can come from a store-bought brand. Many of us just want to find a bra that fits our temple perfectly.

The point is that your body is yours. You're in control over what goes in your body, what you put on it, and how you present it to the world. Keep that in mind as you read this chapter. It's all about how to make the best choices we can for our bods—but you gotta do you. So whether it's picking out the right shade of lipstick or getting better at napping, only you will know what's best for your bod. If you've ever wondered how to give yourself a breast exam, whether or not to shave your bikini line, or how to put on eyeliner without poking your own eye out, then read, read, and read! If you don't shave or wear eyeliner, then skip those entries. (But please still give yourself a breast exam, or make sure you're getting them on the regular from your doctor!)

No matter who you are, remember that you only get this one body. Keep treating it like the temple it truly is.

1 FIND THE RIGHT-FITTING BRA

If anything should be there to support you, it's your bra. When you have an important meeting or a hot date or just need a little boost while running errands, your bra should always have your back. However, if you've been feeling less propped up and more bogged down, then it's time to find a new support system.

First of all, a reality check: if buying a bra has always been something of a challenge, you're not alone. Since our body weight tends to fluctuate—even your menstrual cycle can affect the size of your breasts—it makes the search for the right one damn near impossible. There are some methods to ease the madness, though.

When shopping for a bra, start by finding the right band size first, and not the cup size. That's because cup sizes are not standard. So the D cup of a 32D is going to be smaller than the cup of a 34D. The band size is the number before the cup size, and if you hone in on the band size first, which is standard, then you'll be more likely to find a bra that actually fits your chest.

To find the ideal band size, try on a few options. You'll know you've found the one when you try the bra on and the band fits snugly on the first clasp row of the bra. If hooking the bra to the second or third row feels borderline uncomfortable, then you're on the right track. Since the band will inevitably stretch with wear, you want to buy a bra that will leave you room to do just that. On that note,

having to clasp your bra to the last row of prongs is also a sign that it's time to invest in a new bra and get a better hold on your girls.

The other fit to worry about is the bra straps. When you look in the mirror, the back of the bra should rest comfortably in the middle of your back and not be hiked up. So adjust the straps accordingly. If the only way the bra fits is if it's hiked up, take that bra off and tell it to take a hike.

It's wise to not be married to your cup size, especially since different brands can vary by cup. What you should look for is a cup that holds you in without having any extra space left. In other words, you want to avoid a bra that's too big. Conversely, if you notice spillage on the sides of the bra, essentially creating a whole new boob, or it's digging into your skin, then you're not wearing the right size as it's too small.

On average, the lifespan of a bra is painfully short—six to nine months. So if you're wearing a bra on the last hook, the cups seem to have lost their shape, or if you've tightened the straps to the point where the back of the bra is riding up, it's time to bid that bra adieu and say hello to a new bra that knows how to support your needs.

Knock, knock. Who's there? Pointy. Pointy who? The pointy end of your underwire cutting into your side.

That joke isn't funny, and neither is the moment when your bra's underwire escapes and decides to poke at your skin. Fortunately, you can stop the joke (and the pain) pretty quickly with the right tools.

As you likely know, the underwire is found under the cup of your bra. After enough use, the fabric around the underwire can give, exposing the wire to your bare skin. Ouch. When that happens, all you need is moleskin and a pair of scissors. Moleskin is traditionally used for your feet, but don't let that deter you, because moleskin provides an adhesive-backed padding that you can use to your bra's benefit.

Start by pushing the underwire back into the hole it popped out of. Then cut a strip of moleskin large enough to cover the hole on your bra. Remove the adhesive backing of the moleskin, and press it firmly over the torn part of your bra. Hold it in place for a few seconds to make

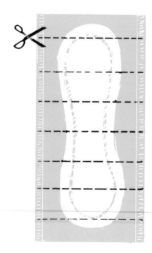

sure it's fully secured, and then you should be ready to put that bra back on your bod.

The moleskin will stay on your bra for as long as you want, so you won't have to throw it out right away. If there's no moleskin around, get a maxi pad and apply it in much the same way. Cut a strip from the pad, so you get some of the padding and adhesive, and apply it over the hole. This is obviously a temporary fix, but one that will definitely do the trick when you need it.

3   GIVE YOURSELF A BREAST EXAM

A mammogram is the best way to catch a lump, but 40 percent of breast cancer cases are found through self-exams. So be the smart woman you are and give yourself a good rubdown so you can keep your ladies healthy.

If you're perpetually short on time, then doing a monthly check while you're in the shower is an easy solution. Using the pads of your fingers, start from the outside of your breast and move in a circular pattern until you reach the center. Check both breasts, as well as your armpits. If you sense a lump, a thicker spot, or a hardened area, then make an appointment with your doctor for a more thorough exam. Don't completely panic if you do feel something unusual. Eight out of ten lumps aren't cancerous, but you won't know until you check with your doctor.

If the shower isn't your favorite place, then lying down in bed is a great way to check for lumps. The bonus here is that you can promptly take a nap when you're done. Start by placing a pillow under the shoulder of the breast you're checking, and raise the arm of that same side above your head. With the opposite hand, use the exact same circular motion you would've used in the shower, starting from the outside and working your way toward the center, to check for any abnormalities. Squeeze the nipple to test for discharge, and repeat on the opposite side.

Yet another option to check for lumps—because options are always a good thing—is to stand in front of your mirror. Raise one arm over your head and use the pads of your fingers to check for lumps and any nipple discharge. When you've completed the test on both sides, stand with your hands on your hips. If you see any bulging of the breast tissue, redness, swelling, or a rash, or if one of your nipples has changed position or suddenly pushed inwards instead of sticking out, then you should schedule an appointment with your doctor for further exams.

Just remember that eight out of ten lumps are benign, and 40 percent of cases are found by a self-exam. So, really, the odds are in your (and your ladies') favor as long as you perform the all-important self-check.

4 CHOOSE THE RIGHT HEELS

It's fair to say that heels are never going to be as comfortable as a pair of fuzzy slippers. But, unfortunately, fuzzy slippers haven't become a totally acceptable shoe to wear out in public. So here are some strategies for all those times when you need to put your best heel forward.

If comfort is your goal, then go for a rounded toe instead of pointed. A pointed toe will press your big toe inward, causing joint pain, whereas a rounded toe allows for more flexibility and room.

And regardless of the shoe's shape, check out the actual heel. The thicker the heel, the more stable you'll be in them. This might explain why stilettos are always such a killer—a skinny heel means less stability! Next look at where the heel of the shoe meets your foot. Is it directly under your heel, or is it at the very back of the shoe? You want to buy a shoe where the heel falls under your own to

provide the most support. A heel placed toward the back won't carry your weight as evenly.

The foundation of any shoe will be its sole, and the thicker the sole the more padding your foot will have each time it lands on the ground. Platforms are great for this, but if it's not a platform, consider adding a gel insert to cushion your foot with each landing. Speaking of landing, you want the sole of the shoe to be made from rubber or leather, either of which has more give than wood or plastic and will result in less pain in the long run. (Not that you should ever run in heels without some practice first.)

Another thing to watch is the back of your heel. Make sure your shoe has some kind of back—a strap or tie that will keep your foot from sliding in and out of the heel. Again, the more stable the shoe, the more stable your feet are, and the less likely you'll be wishing you were back home in those fuzzy slippers.

5   KEEP YOUR VAGINA HEALTHY

Vagina. Honey pot. Snatch. No matter what you call your cookie jar, the truth remains that it's your job to make sure your lady bits stay happy and healthy.

To treat your V right, start by investing in cotton underwear. It allows breathability and absorbs moisture, which will keep your bits dry and prevent infections. Fabrics like nylon trap moisture and make your panties a breeding ground for yeast. At the very least, invest in pairs that offer a cotton strip on the inside to allow that breathing room.

You can also eat right to keep your V happy. Take a probiotic or eat foods like Greek yogurt that are high in active cultures that your lady parts need to fight off infection. Other foods, like avocado, nuts, and olive oil, that are high in vitamin E will help prevent vaginal dryness. And loading

up on cranberries, or cranberry juice, can provide your body with good acids that combat UTIs.

In terms of actually cleaning your vagina, put down the soap and body wash. Your vagina has plenty of mechanisms to help it self-clean, and the only thing you should ever do is wash using warm water, nothing else. Avoid douching at all costs—it takes away the good bacteria from your system.

But it's not just about clothing, nutrition, and hygiene—you can also help your body by doing kegels. Not only does this exercise strengthen your pelvic floor, which can help you achieve stronger orgasms, but a stronger pelvic floor can help prevent ailments like incontinence. So, really, it's a win-win all around. Plus, they're a really simple flex-and-contract exercise that you only need to do three times a week for a minute or two at a time. You're going to squeeze the same muscles that help you stop urinating for ten seconds at a time, with a ten-second break. Squeeze, release. Easiest workout ever.

Speaking of simple steps, when you have sex, know that condoms aren't just about preventing STDs and pregnancy; they also keep your vagina healthy. That's because when semen enters your vagina, it can disrupt the pH levels, leading to bad bacteria. But with a condom, those pH levels stay steady and help prevent UTIs, yeast infections, and bacterial vaginosis.

And of course going for a yearly exam is always a good goal. Much as a visit to the dentist maintains your oral health, with an annual checkup your gynecologist will be able to tell if you're doing everything you can to manage your vaginal health or if other steps can be taken to lead you toward a happier vagina/vag/muffin.

6   FIGHT OFF MENSTRUAL CRAMPS

If anything will give women the advantage when the zombie apocalypse comes, it's that we're able to bleed for a week straight and not complain too much about it. How's that for tough?

So, yeah, we know a thing or two about being fighters. But if you're doubled over in pain, or your cramps seem unusually painful, make an appointment to see a doctor. If you have a normal amount of pain during your period, then these tricks may help you kick extra ass each month (and during the apocalypse).

If there's a bathtub or a heating pad in your home, use them. Heat opens up blood vessels and improves blood flow, which can alleviate the pain. On the opposite end of the spectrum, caffeine constricts blood vessels and slows the flow of blood—causing cramps—so it's best to limit caffeine while you're menstruating.

Over the counter anti-inflammatory drugs that contain ibuprofen or naproxen can also knock out pain if you take them at the first sign of symptoms. But if you'd rather avoid the pain meds, a more natural approach includes loading up on calcium with magnesium, as studies have shown this supplement can help reduce cramps. Need a tastier option? Add cinnamon, ginger, peppermint, or basil to a cup of warm water, as those herbs have shown promise in easing cramps. Plus, those warm liquids may help open up blood vessels.

Finally, there's a long-held belief that exercising can reduce cramps. While there are conflicting studies showing the benefits or lack thereof when it comes to exercising your cramps away, there's no doubt that by exercising you're taking your mind off the pain. Additionally, exercising does release feel-good endorphins that could distract from the pain. So when all else fails, just hop on the treadmill and pretend you're running from the zombies.

7 MAKE YOUR OWN NATURAL DEODORANT

Everyone smells. But a woman who makes her own DIY natural deodorant gets to control what she smells like.

The primary goal of deodorant is to eliminate body odor, so start by finding an essential oil you like the smell of. That oil will determine what your DIY deodorant smells like on you—peppermint, lavender, and lemon are all great options. Once you have your oil, the other ingredients you'll need are coconut oil, baking soda, and cornstarch. (If you have sensitive skin, sub arrowroot powder for the cornstarch and use less of the baking soda, or sub it out entirely for food-grade diatomaceous earth.)

To make the deodorant, take one-half cup of coconut oil and nuke it in the microwave for ten seconds or until it's fully melted. Then add in one-fourth teaspoon of your essential oil and mix until smooth. Next take one-fourth cup of baking soda (or less, if your skin is sensitive) and one-fourth cup of cornstarch (or arrowroot), and blend them into the coconut and essential oil mixture.

Transfer the mixture to an application jar or tube, and refrigerate overnight.

Once the mixture is solid, you'll have your very own DIY deodorant without any of those hidden additives—which is doing something really great for your body.

8 MAKE YOUR OWN HAIR MASK

Do you want the flowing, shimmering locks of a mermaid? Of course you do, so get your hair to smell like the beach and shine like the sun with a homemade hair mask.

While a hair mask may sound tricky, it's one of those wonderful things that's simple to do and ends in a flawless result. All you'll need for this is coconut oil and olive oil. Start by combining a tablespoon of room-temperature coconut oil and half a tablespoon of olive oil in a small bowl. If you run out of the mixture when you apply it, or need more of it, just mix up more—so long as it's two parts coconut oil to one part olive oil, you're golden.

Now apply the coconut mixture to your dry hair, and particularly the dry, damaged ends of your hair. It may seem a little counter to how you normally clean your hair, but you'll want to apply this mask to dry, unwashed hair instead of wet hair. Then wrap your hair in a bun or let it stand on its own, if you have short hair. Best of all? You get to let it soak in for thirty minutes, which means you have a spare half hour to grab a snack, watch TV, or do whatever makes you happy (perhaps sing on a rock, if you're a mermaid hopeful).

When your time is up, hop in the shower and rinse out the coconut mixture. It may feel like it's impossible to get all that oil out of your hair, and that's OK, because you're going to shampoo and condition as you normally would. The shampoo should strip much of the coconut oil out, and you can shampoo twice if your hair is particularly

thick. When your hair dries, you'll notice that it smells like you just stepped off the sand, and looks like you have ocean waves for hair. In a word: mermaid-esque.

9 DIY BODY BUTTER

Anything that contains the word *butter* is a good thing. So butter for your body is a *very* good thing. The cool thing about body butter is that as a DIY, you can add in essential oils to give it whatever scent you like. Plus without all those chemicals, this is a great moisturizer for people with sensitive skin.

You'll want to start by gathering up your ingredients— cocoa butter, shea butter, coconut oil, and olive oil—and put a half cup of each ingredient into a small pot. Combine it all over medium to low heat, stirring constantly until the mixture is fully melted. Once it's melted, remove it from the heat and let it cool for five to ten minutes before placing it in the fridge to chill for an hour. Check it halfway through to see the consistency—your end result should be partially hardened yet still soft.

When the right consistency hits, take the pot out of the fridge and add in fifteen to twenty drops of your

favorite essential oil, like vanilla or lavender. Then, using a hand mixer, whip it all up until the body butter is fluffy and has the consistency of whipped cream.

At this point, you'll want to eat it. But don't do that. Instead, put the mixture in a jar with a lid. If your house stays above 75°F, store it in the fridge. Otherwise, this body butter is ready to be rubbed into your skin.

10 GET BETTER AT NAPPING

Napping is seriously enjoyable. It is also seriously good for your health. Studies have shown that naps can boost your memory, creativity, and mood, and can help you live longer. So if you're clever—and you are—you'll make time to get better at napping (even if it's just on the weekends).

If you're going to bed at a normal hour and waking up at a normal time, then the best napping window is between 1:00 and 3:00 p.m. That's because we get two periods of intense sleepiness every twenty-four hours— between 2:00 and 4:00 a.m., and again between 1:00 and 3:00 p.m. So plan to nap when your body is naturally going to feel tired.

Make sure to set an alarm for your nap so you don't oversleep. Something as quick as a twenty-minute catnap can increase alertness. If you have more time, forty-five minutes is a great goal. Just don't nap any longer than ninety minutes, as that can cause sleep inertia, making you feel groggy.

If you have trouble falling asleep, create an environment that will make napping a whole lot simpler. You want a dark room at a temperature that makes you feel neither too cold nor too hot. If you can, lie down, as trying to fall asleep while sitting will take you 50 percent longer. If there's a lot of noise going on in your 1:00-to-3:00 p.m. window, then invest in earplugs or white noise—even the sound of a fan running will do.

And if you're nervous about being groggy when you wake up, drink a cup of coffee before your nap. It takes caffeine about twenty minutes to kick in, so you can nap and wake up feeling alert and refreshed.

11 SHAVE YOUR BIKINI LINE

These days, if you want to rid yourself of body hair, there are about as many ways to do it as you can dream up. And if you don't want to remove any body hair, you don't have to. What a time to be alive!

Now, for those who do want to get rid of the hair on their bikini line, start by finding the right razor. There are razors specifically made to shave your bikini area, but you

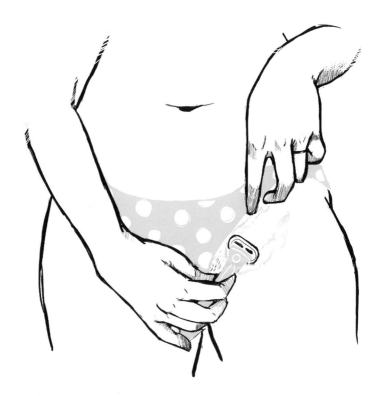

can also find trimmers (even a men's beard trimmer) if you don't want to shave everything off but get close to it.

To make things easier on yourself, trim the hair down there before you get to shaving. Use a pair of scissors and trim everywhere except your labia.

Next hop in the shower or a bath and hang out in the warm water for a solid five minutes. The warm water will soften your skin and make the whole process a lot smoother, no pun intended. When you're ready, apply a fragrance-free shaving cream, and shave in the same direction that your hair grows. This will prevent any ingrown hairs from forming.

As you're shaving, go over the skin gently. Remember that this is your bikini area, so you want to be extra careful and not press down on the skin too hard—and apply more shaving cream as needed.

When you're all done, pat the area dry with a towel, moisturize with an oil-free moisturizer, and wear cotton underwear to limit the likelihood of irritation.

12   GET RID OF AN INGROWN HAIR

Red, inflamed, and painful. No, this isn't describing your last breakup, it's an ingrown hair. Though, much like a bad ex, ingrowns are difficult to get rid of.

The best way to avoid ingrown hairs is to avoid shaving, so let this be your get-out-of-shaving pass, if you wanted one and didn't have one already. However, if shaving is your thing, then you probably want to know how to deal with the angry little bumps that pop up around your armpits, bikini area, and legs. (Seriously, just leave us alone, ingrowns!)

First things first: when you do shave, always shave in the direction that the hair grows, as this will help prevent ingrown hairs from happening. After shaving, exfoliate your skin with a salt or sugar scrub. And when you're coming out of the shower, end by gently patting yourself dry. You don't want to irritate the area you just scraped clean of hair further, so no rubbing your towel around where you shaved.

When you do get an ingrown hair, the big thing is to not pick at it with your fingers. It can be tempting, but this can lead to infection and cause even more pain. Instead, apply an acne cream with benzoyl peroxide to the bump. The cream will reduce inflammation and allow the ingrown hair to grow outward, instead of inward. You'll also want to gently exfoliate around the ingrown hair to slough off dead skin and allow it more room to grow outward.

In most cases an ingrown hair will clear itself up, especially if you don't pick at it. But if it's clear the hair is near the surface, then you can use a pair of sterilized tweezers to gently remove it. Much like the don't-pick-at-the-bumps rule, you don't want to try and tweeze out a hair that isn't near the surface. If it's not ready for removal, just sit tight and wait for the ex—er, ingrown—to move on.

13   AVOID CHAPPED LIPS

Like the deserts miss the rain, your lips miss the moisture they had before they got chapped.

If you're prone to chapped lips, then avoid long-lasting lipsticks that have ingredients that will dry out your lips. Instead opt for creamier lipsticks that, while they might need to be applied more often, will continue to hydrate your lips. And whenever you buy a lip balm, make sure that shea or beeswax is a key ingredient so it nourishes your lips.

The ultimate rule is that if your lips are starting to feel dry, don't lick them. Saliva dries out your lips, which is a cruel trick of our bodies. On that same moisture note, make sure to keep chugging water so you aren't dehydrated. (If you're sensing a moisture theme here, then you're absolutely correct.)

Even with all those precautions, sometimes lips still get chapped. When that happens, use a lip exfoliator to clear away the dead skin cells and make room for the new soft ones. You can also take vitamin B12, which has been shown to help keep your lips hydrated. If none of these strategies is helping, then the problem may not be your lips and could instead be that the air in your home is dry. If that's the case, invest in a humidifier that will provide some much-needed moisture and take away that Sahara vibe.

14 CLEAN YOUR MAKEUP BRUSHES

When the time comes for your close-up, you'll want a strong team of makeup brushes by your side. But did you know your makeup brushes absorb all kinds of bacteria and oils? It's gross, but true, since you rub them on your face on the regular!

Learning how to clean your brushes will ensure that you're always camera ready without the bacterial hangers-on. All you need to clean your tools is some baby shampoo or a mild liquid soap. You'll pour a bit of the shampoo into the palm of your hand and mix it up with warm water. Then take your brush and swirl it in the warm soapy water that's in the cup of your hand. This should work up a lather, at which point you can run the brush under clean, warm water. If the water from the brush looks dirty as you rinse it off, then repeat the swirl and-lather until the water runs clean. Clean water equals a clean makeup brush.

Then use a paper towel or a cloth to dry the brush, starting from the base of the brush and wiping up toward the ends, reshaping the bristles as you go. After that, all you have to do is let the brush air-dry on a towel.

A dermatologist would likely advise you clean a brush after every use to really avoid those excess germs, but if the idea of that is too daunting, once a week or once every other week is a good amount to aim for. Don't think of it as cleaning but more as a treat for your face.

15   FIND THE RIGHT LIPSTICK

While you may have much to learn, you, too, can become the next lipstick master, young grasshopper. Perfect pouts don't have to just be something you see on other people.

To become a true master, think about the texture of a lipstick when you're shopping around. There's sheer, satin, matte, or gloss. Both sheer and satin lipsticks will provide more moisture for your lips and go on a bit shinier, but they will need to be touched up more frequently. Matte, on the other hand, lacks the moisture of a satin and sheer, but has a natural finish and tends to last for a bit longer. A gloss typically is the easiest to apply, adds moisture, and definitely provides the most shine out of all the options. Make sure to buy a gloss with an SPF, as gloss can actually absorb and attract more sun than you need, leading to premature skin aging and potentially skin cancer. So decide which texture would be best for your master skills, and proceed from there.

Next, think about the color. If you want more of a neutral color, then don't go more than a few shades lighter or darker than your natural lip color. When choosing a brighter shade of lipstick, go for a color based on your

skin tone. For darker skin tones, you can really experiment with deep and rich hues, like berries and reds. Olive complexions are fairly neutral, but if you want bold you can't go wrong with a warm plum color. To play off of a fair skin tone, think roses and pinks, or even a bright red to contrast with your skin. And know that there's no wrong shade for you—pick whatever you're drawn to and try it out. If you hate it, then it's on to the next color.

Once you have your lipstick, it's time to apply it. If what you're working with is a bold hue, then dab some concealer or foundation on the skin around your lips. It will help keep your color in place and provide some contrast to the bright color. Once the shade is on, you can clean up the edges with a lipstick pencil, which will also keep the color from bleeding. As a final step, any true master lipstick wearer will tell you to insert your index finger in between your lips and slowly pull it out to make sure none of the color winds up on your teeth. Next thing you know it'll be lights, camera, action!

16 APPLY EYELINER WITHOUT POKING YOUR EYE OUT

What if there were a way to apply eyeliner without the threat of an ER visit? Or, to be less dramatic, without any risk of getting stuff in your eyes?

To get started, find the right eyeliner for you; there's liquid, which is made for its precision; pencil, which is the easiest to apply, but often doesn't spread as thickly as other liners; and gel, which has a matte finish and glides on easily. If you're a beginner, then a pencil may be a good option, but if you want a thicker liner that pops, gel or liquid is best.

When applying your liner, resist the urge to pull on the skin at the outside corners of your eyes—that will just

TAPE

ADD ✶ EYELINER

✶ REMOVE TAPE ✶

DONE!

irritate your face. Instead, try to sit in front of a mirror and rest your arm on a table so you can steady your hand. As you draw on the liner, place your pinky on your cheek to stabilize that arm as much as possible. The steadier the hand, the fewer chances for mistakes.

If you're new to liquid liner and feel a little skittish, start by making dots or dashes along your lash line. Depending on the shape of your brush, you'll know which shape will be easier to make. Once you have the dots or dashes, connect them with the liner and then let your line dry.

Another easy trick is to add a winged corner to each eye, which looks like a subtler cat eye. To do that, take a piece of scotch tape and apply it at an angle to the corner of each eye. You'll draw over the top edge of the tape with your liner, essentially using the tape as a guide. It may seem a little odd, but it's an easy way to ensure you won't get eyeliner smudged everywhere. When you've drawn on the wing, remove the tape and admire that perfectly gorgeous eye.

If you do get eyeliner smears, don't lose your nerve. There are a few easy fixes, like dabbing a cotton swab in concealer and going over the smudged area. The concealer will hide the mistake and allow you to shape the liner as you go. Or if you dip a cotton swab in petroleum jelly, you can run it along the smudge to correct it. If the line looks a little jagged, you can easily smooth it out by going over your line in the same color eyeshadow.

17 GIVE YOURSELF A MANICURE

If you're in the market for beautiful nails but are short on time, money, and patience, then an at-home mani is the perfect solution.

This may seem obvious, but shaping your nails should happen before the manicure. So deciding on a shape for your nails is a great place to start. Whether it's oval or square, that choice will give you some direction when you file and trim.

Before you load on the polish, take a cotton swab dipped in petroleum jelly and go along the skin that borders your nail. It'll prevent the polish from getting on your skin, and will make for super easy cleanup.

When you're ready to paint, start with a base coat on just the tips of your nails, then let that dry and apply a full base coat. The initial coat combined with the second will keep your nails from chipping. Once the base is dry, it's time to get your color game on. Roll the bottle between your palms instead of shaking it, which can cause bubbles in the polish. When the polish is ready, put a drop in the center of your nail, just above the cuticle. Push the drop down with your brush toward the cuticle, then pull it back

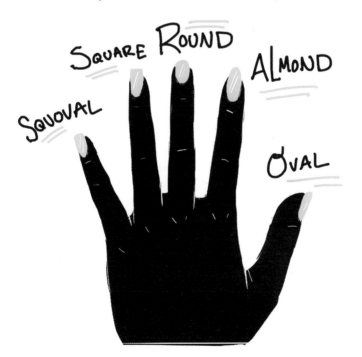

SQUARE ROUND ALMOND
SQUOVAL
OVAL

up to the tip of the nail in a straight line. Go back to the base of the nail and pull your brush up along the right side of the nail, then back to the base to cover the left side of the nail, until your nail is evenly coated.

One of the great things about a mani at home is that you get to control how long it takes. If time is an issue, you can dip your hand in ice water for thirty seconds to help the polish dry faster. Or if the cold water is too . . . cold, another quick-dry option is to spritz a nonstick cooking spray onto your finished nails, let it set for a few minutes, then wash the spray off your hands.

18 GET PERFECT EYELASHES

Maybe she's born with it, or maybe she just knows every little technique to applying mascara. Either way, you can be privy to those tricks too.

First of all, buy a mascara that has the same lash goals as you. There are volumizing, curling, lengthening, and waterproof mascaras. If you want to plump your lashes, go for volumizing; if you want them a little more natural but still looking long, get lengthening; and so on.

If you plan to use an eyelash curler, make sure to use the curler before the mascara. While you may have seen people pumping their mascara wands inside the tube before the application, you don't want to do that. It causes the mascara to clump and invites bacteria into the tube. Yikes. Instead, twirl the wand inside the tube before you take it out, and wipe off any globs onto a tissue.

When you apply the mascara, if you want to thicken your lashes, give the top row a double coat and sweep from right to left before sweeping up to the tips of your lashes.

Getting mascara on your bottom lashes is a whole lot trickier than the top ones because they're shorter, and poking yourself in the eyeball is a high probability. So if

that's been a problem, roll out mascara onto a piece of tissue, then take a small brush, like a lip brush (clean it beforehand), and apply the mascara directly starting at the roots of your bottom lashes and sweep down.

If your mascara seems a little clumpy, there are two ways to fix it. One is to get a cup of warm water and soak the mascara tube for a few minutes. This will make the formula thinner and easier to apply. Similarly, you can add a few drops of saline solution to your mascara tube to thin out the formula and nix flakes. Now when you go out with your new lashes, others may just think you were born with them, and you can totally keep it that way.

be a boss

YOU DON'T NEED a corner office, a tailored blazer, or even the title of *boss* to be a boss. You just need to be a woman who knows what she wants and isn't afraid to go out and get it. Which describes you to a *T*, right?

Look, even if you have no idea what you want, that's OK. The truth is that most people don't have their lives together. And sometimes knowing what you want is just as hard as asking for it (especially when it comes to your finances and career). So if you're a woman who doesn't totally feel like a boss yet, don't panic. It takes time, dedication, and the drive to better yourself, which isn't something that always comes naturally. Luckily, there are easy ways to be more assertive and take some steps in the right direction.

The pages that follow will give you plenty of skills to take yourself to the next level. By the end of this chapter, you won't be worrying about whether you'll get a raise, because you'll know how to negotiate one. And when it comes to your money and how to make it grow, you'll have the stock market on lock. Before you know it, it'll be time to think about buying a home, and you'll be the smart woman who knows the ins-and-outs of a mortgage. So when it's time to retire, you won't have to worry—you'll have been investing toward your future for years.

Not knowing what to do about your career and money stops now. And that's the first step to being a boss.

1   WRITE AN AWESOME COVER LETTER

They say you can't judge a book by its cover, but someone is definitely going to judge you on your cover letter. So instead of phoning it in, make sure to take the time to write a decent one.

Before you get to writing, do a little research on the company you're applying to. You'll be better able to grasp what the company's mission is by looking for an "about" page on its website, and if it has social media, you can see what it's willing to share with the rest of the world. Doing five minutes of legwork will make for a more personalized and attention-grabbing letter.

And just because it's a letter doesn't mean you have to start it off with a "Dear hiring manager" boilerplate. If you have no clue who will be reading it, then nix the "To whom it may concern" and start in on the real meat of the letter.

The real meat comes in the first paragraph, which is where you'll either hook an employer or force the person to read the next candidate's letter. You want to open with a punch, and skip the "I'm applying to the (insert job title here) position at your company" line. Instead, state up front why you're a great fit for this position and why you're excited to be applying. So instead, kick the letter off with something like "I'm a skilled technician with five years of experience, and I know how to bring your company's infrastructure to the next level, which I'll discuss in more detail." You want to be specific in that first paragraph, and if you happen to know someone at the company, definitely drop that name, as it will give you a leg up on the competition.

In your second paragraph, resist the urge to regurgitate what's already in your resume. Instead, use that space to show what an expert you are in your field. So, if you're applying for a job in marketing, talk about how exciting it was to start new initiatives at your last job, or what changes you've seen in the field that you want to explore more at this company.

Remember, a cover letter should be short and sweet, so keep it to three paragraphs tops. Use the last paragraph to convey your enthusiasm about this job and the value you'll bring to it. If you convey that well, the employer will see exactly how valuable you are.

2 ACE A JOB INTERVIEW

There are plenty of candidate fish in the sea. So the real trick of any job interview is, how do you become the fish they want to reel in?

When you schedule the interview, try to make it on the earlier side, as studies have shown that interviews that happen in the morning tend to go better than those that happen later in the day. And maybe you've been told this before, but dress to impress. Even if you know the company you're interviewing with has a laid-back culture, as someone aspiring to have a job there, it's important that you put some effort into your look. Aim for business casual, at a minimum, and avoid the just-rolled-out-of-bed look.

While your resume and experience obviously play a role in whether you'll be walking through that company's doors on a regular basis, the real sell you have to make is that you'd be a great cultural fit. That means that the most important part of the interview is to prove that

you're a likable person. You can do that by mirroring the interviewer's demeanor. Is the person very laid-back or screaming professionalism? Read the interviewer's body language and tone, and try to mirror that as best you can.

And because you need that likability factor, you want to make sure that your shining personality comes across too. So when appropriate, don't hesitate to crack a joke. If there's an opportunity to share a personal story, keep it short and sweet, but do share it. You want the interviewer to leave the room feeling as if you could be a friend.

Something else to keep in mind is that while you'll be asked a lot of questions, you should come prepared with plenty of questions of your own to ask. You should bring a pen and notebook and be prepared with five to ten questions about the company. You can ask about the hardest part of the job, the best part of the job, what the company culture is like, and if there's a vision for growth. The only question to avoid in the initial interview should be salary—save that for follow-up interviews and discussions with the HR department.

Strike a pose. No, we're not vogueing—we're learning an amazing tool that will help you and the rest of the world view you as a stronger and more empowered woman.

If you're closed up, wrapping your arms around your body, shrinking in on yourself, and making yourself smaller in general, you're taking on a low-power pose. But when you open up your body, stand tall, or lean forward, you're in a high-power pose. And research has shown that when you take on power stances, or even do a power pose for two minutes before an important event, you're more likely to be confident, feel less stress, and be more secure in taking risks. This translates to you feeling and looking more like a boss in the long run.

When you have a big meeting coming up, an interview, or hell, even a first date, prep for it by doing a high-power pose. That means you should stand up tall, raise your hands over your head, and spread your feet wide. Open up your body and hold that pose for two minutes. If you're seated, or unable to stand, put your hands behind

↑ HIGH POWER ↑

LOW POWER

your head and open your arms so you can feel the full expanse of the move without getting up.

And in your everyday work life, assume a power pose for meetings and when talking to coworkers. Lean forward, keep your arms open and relaxed, sit with your legs apart, and maintain open posture. The more space you take up, the more power and presence you have in a room. The moral here is that if you act powerful, you will be powerful, and others will perceive you as such too.

4 NEGOTIATE YOUR SALARY

No one's going to show you the money unless you ask for it. And it's universally true that asking for a higher salary can be super scary. But if you don't ask for it, the scarier reality is you won't be making as much as you could. Studies have shown that women are significantly less likely to negotiate than men are, so if for no other reason, negotiate so that women can close the pay gap.

To know how much you should be earning, you need to do your homework. There are several websites that list the average income for certain positions by city, so you can make a comparison. You should also reach out to friends in similar fields and get a range as to what they're making. Then you'll want to pick the top number of that range. So say you get a range of $50,000 to $55,000. You're going to pick $55,000, because you're a smart and valuable woman who's entitled to the top of that range. Also, research has shown that picking a very specific number makes recruiters assume you've done your home-work, which means you're more likely to get you what you want. So you'd want to say that your price is $55,000, as opposed to a range between $50,000 and $55,000.

So now you know your value, which means when the call comes in, you're going to be prepared. You can and should let them make an offer, unless the hiring manager explicitly asks you for one. An offer is just that—the first

step toward a bigger negotiation. Most offers come in at average or slightly below to leave wiggle room for negotiations, so you should absolutely push back against a first offer, even if it feels awkward to do so. Something as simple as, "I'm so excited to work here, and I know that my unique skills will bring this company to a new level. I appreciate the offer of $48,000 but was really expecting to be at $55,000 based on my experience. Can we talk about a salary of $55,000 for this?"

Just remember that no one is going to show you the money unless you ask for it, and if all else fails, you can always yell, "Show me the money!" (It worked for Tom Cruise, after all.)

5   NEGOTIATE A RAISE

Money makes the world go round, and since you're the queen of your world, it's time to take what's yours.

So, on to the hard part: the asking. The asking *will* be hard, if only because asking anyone for money—whether it be your boss or your parents—isn't always the easiest of scenarios. It should be stressed that the worst-case scenario is that they say no. The best case, however, is that because you asked for a raise, you get one, and your life becomes a whole lot more plentiful. To get things started, prepare your boss for what you want to talk about by scheduling a meeting and being clear that you'd like to discuss your performance and salary. Or, if you have reviews coming up, let your boss know through email or in person that you'd like to discuss salary. This will put your boss in the right headspace for the discussion and also provide time to think what number to offer you.

Because you're a very prepared person, go into the meeting with a running list of all your accomplishments since your last raise. The easiest way to keep track of this is throughout the months between discussions—either in a document or in a weekly email you send to yourself. Keeping track of your achievements, big and small, will help you to come up with a list of reasons why you deserve this raise. Think of those reasons in terms of personal accomplishments, ways you've influenced others, your team's accomplishments, and what your plans are for the months ahead.

Before you go to the meeting, have a number in mind that you want to ask for. If, for whatever reason, your boss says no to your raise, that doesn't mean you should give up. The company wants you to stay; otherwise you'd be let go. So you can ask for other things—more paid time off, more job responsibilities, and so on. And ask for the specific steps you need to take in order to be considered for a raise next time. A no is the worst-case scenario, but you should always strive to get what you deserve.

6 STOP SAYING "SORRY"

End your sorry streak and stop apologizing for things that don't require one. You know, like saying "Sorry" anytime you ask a question, speak your mind, or walk into a room. Sorry, but does that sound familiar at all? (See what happened there?)

It's important to know that every time you use that word when it isn't required, it puts you at a disadvantage. That's because you immediately become the subservient person in that situation. By saying "Sorry," you're relinquishing some of your strength, and as a leader that's something you definitely don't want to do.

The fact that you're reading this means you're already becoming more aware of your language. But going forward, be mindful of the words you're using. If you catch yourself saying "Sorry," make a note of it, drop a dollar in a jar, or do whatever you have to do in order to make yourself stop saying it. If you need more help, tell a friend or coworker that every time you say "Sorry," they have to point it out. Being aware of what you're saying will help you correct the problem.

If it's still an issue, then find a substitute phrase to use. Maybe it's *OK* or *Let me say*. Even a *Sorry, not sorry* will do. Because in order to be perceived as a strong leader, you have to ban that word from your language. (Unless, of course, you actually do need to apologize for something, in which case you get a free *sorry* pass.)

7 START SAYING "NO"

If you're the type who breaks out in a sweat whenever someone asks if you want to hang out, then breathe easy: saying "No" doesn't make you a bad person. It just makes you a more direct one and, in that way, there's a lot of power in a *no*.

So to embrace the word *no*, let's first let go of the notion that people will hate you if you say it. Here's the thing: if someone is asking for a favor, or even asking you to attend an event, it means they're asking for your time. Which means they're asking for your permission. If, for example, your friend asks if you can be her plus one to an event, and you don't want to attend, that's perfectly reasonable—it's a favor for her, so saying "No" just means she'll ask someone else. No harm, and no reason for anyone to hate you.

Make sure to tell people your answer quickly, and don't leave them hanging. Again, people won't hate you for declining, but they will resent the fact that you waited until the last possible moment to do so. So respect their time, and tell them as soon as you can. When you do say

"No," be prepared to explain why. This doesn't mean you have to make up some insane reason as to why you can't go, or use the "I'm sick" excuse. You can say something as simple as "I've had a super busy week, and I need a night in" and leave it at that.

If you want to go above and beyond, then you can also offer the person an alternative solution. Maybe you know someone who would want to go, or you would be willing to do what they're asking at a later date. Whatever it is, if you have a different way to accomplish the person's goals, feel free to present it. Since there's no need to sweat a *no*, now you can get on the road to embracing it.

8 DELIVER CONSTRUCTIVE FEEDBACK

Break out the notepad and hike up the big-girl pants, because it's time to learn how to deliver constructive feedback.

If you see a behavior that needs to be changed with a coworker you want to say something within a day. In other words, don't wait a week to tell a person they made a mistake; you should give that feedback while the behavior is still a fresh memory. Aim to address it the next day, and set a meeting with a specific agenda. Something like "Hey, I'm setting a meeting to discuss something I noticed in your presentation today." You want the person to be as mentally prepared as you are.

When you're face-to-face with the person you're giving feedback to, be direct and honest about the issues. Avoid attacks on personality or insults to the person's capabilities. Instead, address the behavior that needs to change. So, instead of "That email you sent was really stupid," a better approach would be "We need to be more thoughtful with subject lines when we're emailing clients." Keep your tone honest, not accusatory, and the person will be much more receptive.

A much harder situation is when you're not a huge fan of the person you're giving feedback to. Regardless of your personal feelings, it's important to treat the person with respect. Imagine this is a different colleague—your favorite—so that when you deliver the feedback, it's exactly how you'd deliver it to a person you really like. This will help you avoid being petty and will give the person less of a reason to be defensive.

Then offer an opportunity to provide feedback for you. When you're done explaining the issue, you can ask, "How do you think we should handle this going forward?" The person will be able to discuss any obstacles and will also feel empowered with a voice.

Throughout the conversation, be sure to couple the negative with positive feedback about how that employee is doing overall. And at the end, you want to leave with an action plan, or the promise of making one. It should be on you to decide what needs to change moving forward, and how to make that happen, but collaborating on that in any way will make the person feel like part of the solution.

9   HANDLE TOUGH CRITICISM

Everybody hurts at times—and one of those times is when you receive less-than-glowing feedback.

But here's the thing to keep in mind when your employer (or even a friend) tells you that things need to change: this is an opportunity. Not only are you being told there's a problem, you're being told that a person has faith that you're able to handle this feedback and learn from it. Because you're a hard-working person, you will take that criticism and grow, showing that you can navigate situations like this.

That being said, the first thing to do when you receive constructive criticism is to pause and not react defensively. Don't deflect the blame or argue what a person is saying. Instead just listen, take it in, and even let yourself be hurt. Just remember that someone is giving you feedback because they want you to improve and not to bruise your ego.

You'll also need to listen carefully to what's being said. Often we can tune out negativity, but in this instance it's important to understand what needs to be changed. If

personal
GROWTH
plant

the person delivering feedback is being vague, or you're uncertain of what the issue really is, ask for explanation. "Just to clarify, you need me to handle X differently, right?" is an easy way to confirm what changes you're being asked to make.

After the conversation, you should discuss the criticism with your friends or close coworkers. Go through what you were told with others, and assess their thoughts on whether what's being asked is reasonable. Because you're a smart woman, you'll want to follow up with the person who gave you this feedback. Be respectful and kind in your response. "Thank you so much for your thoughts; they make a lot of sense to me, and I want to make sure we're on the same page" is a great way to start. Then restate the changes you're expected to make and express any concerns you have around them. If you need help making those changes, be vocal about it. If you think some of the expectations are unreasonable, politely express that.

Just remember that you have the capacity to grow and learn from feedback. Criticism is how we get better at our jobs and our personal lives, so know that it's coming from a desire for improvement, rather than negativity.

10 LEAVE A JOB ON GOOD TERMS

If only leaving a job could be as easy as an Irish goodbye—you'd quietly pack your belongings into a box and, while everyone else is busy listening to some presentation, you walk out the doors and never see them again.

Alas, there's that pesky two-weeks notice standing between you and that dream. Furthermore, you probably want to leave your job on good terms, which means no sudden movements and playing it cool even though you may be itching to leave.

So first things first: provide enough notice. Two weeks is never really enough time to find a replacement, but it is the standard, so give two weeks, or more if you can. You may need this company to provide a reference for you further down the road, so make sure your boss is the first person you tell, and be modest about your new job. The reason you're getting that shiny new salary is because you were at this job, being nurtured and primed by your coworkers—so keep that in mind.

While you're in the awkward middle zone that is still being employed at this company while waiting to move on to the next one, be sure that you continue performing at your peak. Your employer will remember your last two weeks the most vividly, so simply checking out or deciding that you no longer need to do work aren't the behaviors you want to leave them with.

If you have the time, try to make your transition as smooth as possible. Maybe it's creating a document describing all the duties that someone else will take on, or writing up a training manual for your replacement—whatever you can do to help the transition will be remembered. It's not as quick as an Irish goodbye, but you'll be glad you took the right steps down the line.

11 COMPLETE A TAX RETURN

You've reached peak adulthood when you learn how to file your taxes without having to use one of your lifelines.

Actually, despite how much people joke about the complexity, it's not as hard as it seems. That's particularly true if you have one source of income and that job required you to fill out a W-4 form. That means taxes are regularly taken out of your paycheck, and filing through an online service is all you'll need to do—no tax professional needed. You'll find most online services are extremely easy to use, and some of them are also free. Now, if you have multiple sources of income, are self-employed, or have loads of investments you're making, then hiring a tax preparer is the way to go.

Regardless of which method you choose, there are a few pro tips to keep in mind. For example, if you want more money back on your return, that means you need to have fewer exemptions on your W-4 tax form. The more exemptions you put, the less money will be withheld from your checks, so if you put fewer exemptions, more will be taken out up front, and you'll get a bigger return. If you're in college, there are tax credits you can take advantage of to ease the financial burden. The American Opportunity Tax Credit gives you $2,500 toward the cost of tuition, fees, and course materials, while the Lifetime Learning Credit gives you $2,000 toward undergrad and graduate expenses if you're enrolled at an eligible school (eligible schools are listed on the IRS website). Or if you've

relocated for a job in the past year and had to pay money to do so, you can use that to your advantage and deduct those expenses. All charitable donations are tax-deductible, so keep track of those.

Above all, if you plan to apply for credits or want anything itemized, start saving your receipts. They'll serve as your proof and will also make entering the data on your return significantly easier. Plus, you're definitely a true adult when you have a folder filled with receipts. Just saying.

12   INVEST YOUR MONEY

Ah, the sweet taste of knowing you won't be living in your parents' basement when you're sixty. All it takes is some planning.

First off, you should know that there's no "right" time to start investing your money. Even if you're not making much, squirreling away what you can now will make a big difference in the long run. There are two easy things that can jump-start your savings plans. The first is to build up an emergency fund, which should be enough cash to last you six months, should anything bad happen (for example, you lose your job or need a new car). Once you've saved enough for the emergency fund, make a financial plan for yourself.

A financial plan boils down to where you're at now, where you want to be, when you want to get there, and how you plan to make that a reality. So look at the now—what you spend, what you could cut back on to save more, and anything you've already saved. Then plan out the next step, or where you want to be. This should be figuring out how much money you need to live your ideal future life. There are tons of online calculators that can help you sort out what you'll need to save, spend, and make to get there.

Once you know where you want to be and what you need to get there, it's time to learn all about investing. Start at your employer—if they offer a 401(k) matching program, absolutely invest in it. If they don't, consider an individual retirement account, or IRA. You'll also want to do your homework on options outside of work. Mutual funds can be a lower-risk investment; they invest in multiple securities, and if one security falls, the others will likely cushion it. A Roth IRA is a great option if you're looking to save money and have the option to take it out, risk-free, at any time. The stock market can be a fun place to dabble, and there are plenty of online tools to prep you before you buy.

Whatever you decide to invest in, just remember that this is an investment toward your future. You may not see big payoffs within a year, and there's always risk involved. However, chances are you'll look at the same account in ten years and the money you put away will have grown and will continue to grow.

After reading that last entry, you may be thinking, "What is the stock market, anyway?" In short, it's a place where you can buy and sell shares of publicly traded companies. While there's always risk involved in investing in a company, think of it this way: since you invest in shares of particular companies, it's rare to lose all your money unless a company goes completely bust. Your money may go down or up, but you will only rarely lose it all. Start small if you prefer, but try not to be completely scared away by the idea of losing money.

In terms of what makes the price of a stock go up or down, it's not simply that the company is doing well or poorly. It can be caused by anything from natural disasters to the media to political unrest. The market can be hard to predict, and things like national crises are impossible to foresee. But markets fall when buyers catch wind of these issues. So the more people selling shares means the more likely it is for those shares to fall. And vice versa: the more people buying means the higher the stock will be valued at. It's supply and demand in action.

Getting cold feet? Stop thinking about it as betting on companies as if you're betting on horses. That's possible, sure (just look at the lucky folks who bought Apple stock decades ago!), but it's not how most people invest. The name of the game is to diversify your investments so you don't have too much money in one particular area. Because stocks are risky, you'll want to be cautious and not have all your money tied to the fate of one company.

Again, in as few words as possible, this is why one of the most common ways to invest is not directly in companies but in index funds managed by investment companies. These funds are diverse and track with a large part of the market. Thus, only a small portion of your money is in the stocks of each individual company within the fund. The investment company can help you pick the fund with the right level of risk for your age and financial situation.

14 ESTABLISH A CREDIT RECORD

You have to give credit where credit is due. But what if you have no credit history?

If you're wondering what a credit history is, it's a record that shows whether you've been responsible with your finances. You've paid off bills in a timely manner, and therefore you have great credit. Or you've neglected to pay bills on time and therefore have a terrible credit history. The problem is establishing a credit history; it can be a catch-22. Even if you've paid all your bills and been responsible with your money, if you don't already have a credit card, you have little to no official history. But to get a credit card, you'll often need said history. So, how do you get past this tricky situation?

The answer for some lies in a secured credit card, which requires a security deposit but will help you establish your initial credit. To establish credit and history, use your card regularly, and keep the account open for as long as possible (again, it's all about that history). Keep your card balance low, and don't let it exceed your monthly limit. And, above all else, pay that bill on time each and every month! When you've built some history, apply for an unsecured credit card, which won't require a deposit and will come with a higher limit and potentially other perks.

If you want to establish credit without a card, there are some other options. You can take out a small personal loan, maybe for a project or for buying a large item like a car, and make the payments in a timely manner every month. In a similar vein, taking out a student loan or credit-builder loan and making your payments punctually will also help establish credit.

Regardless of which direction you go, always pay your bills on time! You'll be well on your way to establishing that credit history and, before you know it, you'll be getting your due credit.

15 RESPECT YOUR FRIENDS' MONEY

What might be the beginning of a beautiful friendship can often derail the minute money enters the equation.

Whether you're making more than your friends or you happen to be the have-not in this scenario, there are ways to navigate these waters without muddying the friendship.

If you're making more money than a friend, the first thing to recognize is that you should always have your friend's best interest at heart. So it's important to understand that while you may want a trip to Napa Valley, your friend may not be able to afford it. If you know for sure a friend can't afford something, suggest an affordable activity. So instead of a wine tour, offer a girls' day where you watch movies and split a bottle of wine. Similarly, if you're the friend on a budget, it's perfectly acceptable to say, "I can't afford that, but I'd still love to do something."

Another issue that can arise is the temptation to borrow and loan money. It might start with you covering the price of drinks at a happy hour. Or maybe you asked your friend to cover concert tickets with the promise of repayment. These situations can often lead to resentment if not handled correctly. If you're the person earning a higher income and your friend asks for money, just know that if you aren't comfortable never seeing that money again, you shouldn't do it. Always go into a loan situation assuming you won't be repaid. If that makes you uncomfortable, all you need is a polite excuse—say you have to pay your rent and can't afford it, or you have a trip coming up. Whatever you say, just don't loan the money if it makes you uncomfortable.

If you're asking for a loan, respect the fact that your friend is allowed to decline. Just because someone is earning more doesn't make the person a piggy bank. If your friend agrees to loan you money, then make a deadline for when to repay it, and stick to the deadline. You can even offer to pay your friend back with interest. This may sound formal, but it's a great gesture if nothing else.

16 SAVE FOR SOMETHING IMPORTANT

What would you buy if you won the lottery? Chances are you already know, because fantasizing about what you'd have if only you had the money is an ancient pastime. But here's the thing: you don't need to wait for the magic numbers to be called to buy something big—just start saving so you can make your fantasy a reality.

Start by setting a goal—not just for the thing you want, but for how quickly you want to achieve it. Say you want to take a fancy weekend getaway, and you've calculated that it will cost $2,000. If you want to take that weekend within six months, then you know you have six months' worth of paychecks to save up the money. If you get paid twice a month, that's twelve checks the money needs to come out of. So you'd divide the total cost you're saving for ($2,000) by the number of checks you'll be getting (twelve), and see that you need to put away $167 each time a paycheck comes in.

If the amount you need to squirrel away each month seems too high for you, then consider extending the time limit for saving what you need. But if you want to stick to the set amount of time, you can also cut down your everyday expenses by doing things like eating in, bringing lunch to work, and skipping the coffee runs. With a little time and saving, you just might get a piece of your fantasy life.

17 BUY A CAR WITHOUT GETTING RIPPED OFF

Walking into a dealership is not unlike stepping in quicksand. Because the longer you're there, and the more you struggle to get out of that sticker price, the faster you end up stuck with a bad deal. Before you know it, you're

buried up to your eyeballs in payments, and you have no idea how you even managed to get there.

Understanding that a dealership is going to try to bury you is the first important step. Because with that knowledge, you can go in armed with the ropes—er, tools—you'll need to stay afloat. The first thing you'll want to do is research before you get close to negotiating. Test-drive cars at multiple lots, compare sticker prices on the exact same models and note the differences, and look up the going prices for cars through online services, like Kelley Blue Book. If you know what you could get at other dealerships, or if the dealer has marked up something substantially, that will give you ammunition when you buy.

With a number in mind, and hopefully a car model in mind, you'll likely move into the paperwork-and-negotiating phase quickly. Many dealers will keep you at a dealership for hours, trying to wear you down or make you so exhausted that you'll sign whatever they put in front of you. The truth is, though, that dealers know if you leave, you're not likely to return. So they want to make a sale while they have you in the room. Bring a friend, and agree that you're leaving after an hour. When that hour comes, get up to go, and you'll be amazed by the deals a salesperson suddenly has to offer.

And the bottom line is that you should read everything thoroughly before buying so you can avoid being tricked into paying hidden fees and costs. It's an annoying reality, but also one you have control over. Once you know where the quicksand in a car dealership is, it's a lot easier to avoid sinking.

18   DONATE TO A GREAT CAUSE

As is the case with most things involving your money, making a donation is something you'll want to research before making a commitment. Is there a cause that's near to your heart? Perhaps you've had a family member who's been ill and you want to donate to charities that deal with that specific illness, or maybe you're partial to your furry friends and prefer an animal charity. Whatever the case, figure out what cause you want to support to narrow the initial search.

Then do some good old-fashioned digging on the internet. There are plenty of resources that examine how much of your donation actually goes to a charity versus

QUESTIONS FOR CHARITY ORGANIZATIONS

· What clear goals does your charity currently have?
· What steps are you taking to make sure you reach those goals?
· What outcomes has the charity already seen through its work?
· How will your donation be used in the charity? (Keep in mind that at least 70 percent of your donation should go toward the cause.)

its overhead, and other sites that evaluate each organization on things like mission and effectiveness. Try to narrow your charity options down to three based on your research, and then move on to the deeper digging.

Now that you have solid options, you either want to meet with a representative from the organization or give them a call to ask more questions. A charitable donation is often tax-deductible, so you can feel free to ask about that too. But the main thing you want to get out of this is that the charity's mission aligns with what you want your money to accomplish, so you can hand off a check and feel great about what it's going toward.

When it comes to a mortgage, you may think you can just cross that bridge when you come to it. But that bridge will likely be here sooner than you expect, and you'll want to know exactly what's coming so that when you cross it, you've got a nice home waiting on the other side.

In the simplest terms, a mortgage is a loan to help finance the purchase of a home. Typically you're expected to put down 20 percent of the cost of the house in cash, and the mortgage covers the rest. So, for example, if you're buying a $200,000 home, you'd need to have $40,000 in cash up front, and your loan would cover the remaining 80 percent of the cost of the home.

When you take on a mortgage, you're typically setting up a fifteen- to thirty-year loan that you'll pay off through monthly payments. You're also agreeing to pay this loan off with interest. As part of signing the mortgage contract, you're also signing the house you bought as collateral. So if payments can't be made, the house serves as your collateral, and the bank has the right to take your house to pay off the mortgage loan. This process is called foreclosure, and it means you'll not only lose the home, but you'll also damage your credit. So before you agree to a mortgage, you should feel secure in your ability to pay it off.

Other costs you'll need to consider before signing a mortgage include interest, which you'll be charged each month you have that loan, taxes (like property taxes), and homeowner's insurance, which you'll need to have in order to buy a home. It's also important to note that when you first start making mortgage payments, you'll pay significantly more in interest than you will further down the line. That's because the interest is calculated off of the current balance due on the home, and the more you repay that mortgage, the less interest you'll owe.

20   ARE YOU READY TO BUY A HOME?

A home of your own might mean no more pesky upstairs neighbors. Or at the very least, it will mean no more landlords who make your blood boil. So, it's a pretty great thing. But as with any big purchase, it's good to take a few things into consideration before you buy.

    You'll likely need to secure financing for your home, so you want to take a good hard look at whether you can afford this purchase in the long run. If you can make the

BE A BOSS

219

monthly mortgage payments, great. But what about other expenses, like moving costs, new furniture, and hidden surprise repairs that inevitably come with a house? Create a budget and allot for home repairs and one major emergency a year, in addition to the mortgage, and see where you land.

You'll also want to consider the stress of owning a home and whether homeownership is worth it for you. In some cities, it's actually cheaper to buy a home than it is to rent, but buying also means that when the plumbing goes askew, it's your job to handle hiring a plumber and the costs that come with it. So just check in with yourself and see if you're up to the task.

And you'll want to think about how long you'd actually live in the house of your dreams, should you find it. How secure are you in your job—and, if hunting together, in your partner's job? Are there other job opportunities in the city you live in should you lose your job? Is the house large enough to accommodate any kids, if that's part of your future? Or would the house make for a suitable rental if you have to move and the market isn't right to sell? Figuring out the answers to these questions will help you figure out whether the house makes sense as an investment.

Last but not least, when it comes to actual house hunting, you want to approach it with a lot of skepticism and ask plenty of questions. If a home has been on the market for some time, is that due to a slow market, a structural or location issue with the home, or is this property overpriced? Similarly, are there any deal-breakers on the house—like a roof that needs to be replaced or issues with the sewage line? Be wary before you buy so you aren't kicking yourself once you have the keys in hand.

Index

ABOUT THE AUTHOR

Erin La Rosa is a writer and performer who received her MA in writing from the University of Southern California and a BA in fiction from Emerson College. Her nonfiction has been published on the website MadAtoms, and her fiction has appeared on Storychord. She's the Los Angeles Bureau Chief for BuzzFeed and frequently writes about food, social skills, how to get ahead in life, and her love of whiskey. Before BuzzFeed, Erin wrote for Funny or Die and E! Online's Fashion Police. One of her passions is storytelling, and she's performed in such series as MORTIFIED, "Funny but True" at the *Los Angeles Times* Festival of Books, and Sunday Night Sex Talks. She enjoys knitting, binge-watching TV with a great pizza, and trying to solve other people's problems. Erin lives in Los Angeles with her husband and their cat, Fish. You can find her on Twitter: @sideofginger.